Station Games

Station Games

Fun and Imaginative PE Lessons

Maggie C. Burk

Human Kinetics

Library of Congress Cataloging-in-Publication Data

Burk, Maggie C., 1970-
  Station games : fun and imaginative PE lessons / Maggie C. Burk
    p. cm.
  ISBN 0-7360-4105-2
    1. Physical education and training--Study and teaching (Elementary) I. Title.

GV363 .B85 2002
372.86--dc21   2001051532

ISBN: 0-7360-4105-2

Copyright © 2002 by Maggie C. Burk

Pages 88 and 92 Adapted, by permission, from B. Wnek, 1992, *Holiday games and activities* (Champaign, IL: Human Kinetics), 70. **Page 98** Reprinted, by permission, from Foster, Hartinger, and Smith, 1992, *Fitness fun* (Champaign, IL: Human Kinetics), 76-77. **Page 116** From G. Graham, S. Holt-Hale, and M. Parker, 1993, "Hit me with your best sit-ups," *Children moving* (Mountain View, CA: Mayfield).

Acquisitions Editor: Amy N. Clocksin; **Developmental Editor:** Jennifer L. Walker; **Assistant Editors:** Susan C. Hagan and Maggie Schwarzentraub; **Copyeditor:** Scott J. Weckerly; **Proofreader:** Susan C. Hagan; **Permission Manager:** Dalene Reeder; **Graphic Designer:** Stuart Cartwright; **Graphic Artist:** Dawn Sills; **Photo Manager:** Leslie A. Woodrum; **Cover Designer:** Keith Blomberg; **Photographer (cover):** Carl D. Johnson; **Art Manager:** Carl D. Johnson; **Illustrator:** Sharon Smith; **Printer:** Versa Press.

Printed in the United States of America   10   9   8   7   6   5   4   3   2   1

Human Kinetics
Web site: www.humankinetics.com

United States: Human Kinetics
P.O. Box 5076
Champaign, IL 61825-5076
800-747-4457
e-mail: humank@hkusa.com

Canada: Human Kinetics
475 Devonshire Road Unit 100
Windsor, ON N8Y 2L5
800-465-7301 (in Canada only)
e-mail: orders@hkcanada.com

Europe: Human Kinetics
Units C2/C3 Wira Business Park
West Park Ring Road
Leeds LS16 6EB, United Kingdom
+44 (0) 113 278 1708

e-mail: hk@hkeurope.com

Australia: Human Kinetics
57A Price Avenue
Lower Mitcham, South Australia 5062
08 8277 1555
e-mail: liahka@senet.com.au

New Zealand: Human Kinetics
P.O. Box 105-231, Auckland Central
09-523-3462
e-mail: hkp@ihug.co.nz

To my parents for always encouraging me to continue my education. They always said that I could do whatever I set my mind to. A special thanks to my husband for his patience, encouragement, and technical support during this project.

Contents

LEGEND

Planning and Set-Up Time

under 15 minutes

15 minutes to 30 minutes

30+ minutes

Equipment Needed

0 to 5 pieces of equipment

5 to 10 pieces of equipment

10+ pieces of equipment

Game Finder

Game title	Planning and set-up time	Equipment needed	Page	Skills
Balance #1	2 clocks	2 cones	23	Coordination and flexibility, fundamental concepts
Balance #2	2 clocks	2 cones	26	Coordination and flexibility, fundamental concepts
Ball-Handling Skills	2 clocks	2 cones	28	Fundamental concepts, sports skills, teamwork and cooperation
Basketball	2 clocks	2 cones	45	Sports skills, teamwork and cooperation
Cardio-Jump	1 clock	1 cone	71	Cardiovascular fitness and endurance, coordination and flexibility
Championship Obstacle Course	2 clocks	2 cones	73	Cardiovascular fitness and endurance, coordination and flexibility
Christmas Cheers	3 clocks	3 cones	91	Cardiovascular fitness and endurance, teamwork and cooperation
Directions, Pathways, and Levels	2 clocks	2 cones	12	Cardiovascular fitness and endurance, coordination and flexibility, fundamental concepts
Field Day	3 clocks	3 cones	107	Cardiovascular fitness and endurance, coordination and flexibility, fundamental concepts, and sports skills
Gymnastics	2 clocks	2 cones	40	Coordination and flexibility, fundamental concepts, sports skills
Halloween Frights	3 clocks	3 cones	88	Fundamental concepts, sports skills, teamwork and cooperation
Healthy Heart Circuits	3 clocks	3 cones	76	Cardiovascular fitness and endurance, cross-curricular study, teamwork and cooperation
Hockey	2 clocks	2 cones	57	Sports skills, teamwork and cooperation
Jumping	2 clocks	2 cones	15	Cardiovascular fitness and endurance, coordination and flexibility, fundamental concepts

(continued)

Preface

According to child researcher and author Shirley Holt-Hale, children learn best from a *reflective* teaching style. This popular teaching method focuses on having teachers use three unique teaching strategies—direct, child-designed, and inquiry—to maximize student understanding. Ideally, according to Holt-Hale, teachers should plan curriculum and lessons that promote opportunities to use these three approaches.

Educators working in traditional classroom settings have been able to successfully employ reflective teaching. Physical educators, however, have found their implementation a challenge because of both the subject matter and the gymnasium environment.

As a physical educator striving for excellence, I have done my homework. I've read the theory, and I've taken the workshops. Through both my studies and teaching experiences, I have found that one of the most effective ways to teach reflectively in the physical education setting is to incorporate learning centers, or *stations*, into classroom planning.

A typical station-based lesson consists of 3 to 10 stations—each station consisting of a single activity contained in a specified area and designed to develop or build skills on an individual or group basis. The learning stations should optimally provide valuable opportunities to introduce students to new skills, to let them practice established skills, and to teach them to work cooperatively with others. From a teaching standpoint, stations can be invaluable tools to observe the class both as a whole and on an individual basis, to accurately assess students' progress, and to prescribe extra practice or give individual instruction.

This book contains my helpful tips and strategies for successfully implementing station lessons into everyday curriculum. It contains glimpses of my experiences as well as over 40 station lessons I've developed throughout the years, complete with step-by-step instructions, objectives, and outcomes. After some introductory remarks in *Teaching Tips* (chapter 1), the lessons are then divided into *Basic Skills* (chapter 2), *Sports Fundamentals* (chapter 3), *Fitness Essentials* (chapter

4), *Themes* (chapter 5), and *Stretches, Tags, and Quick Skills* (chapter 6). They are all presented in a manner that is friendly—and fun—to use. Many of the stations in this book are easily adaptable and can be tailored to your personal classroom dynamics. I encourage you to use the lessons as springboards that encourage you to think *outside the box* when designing station lessons: Think of your own special touches, like music, costumes, catchy titles, and different and unexpected kinds of equipment.

It is my hope that this book helps other teachers to improve both their own teaching styles and the health and physical fitness of the students they teach. Learning stations have made my own teaching style more diverse, my lesson plans more fulfilling, and my student understanding of key skills at its best. Here's to hoping that station lessons bring you these improvements and more!

Acknowledgments

Special thanks to Howell Flatt and Cybil Levy for their professional input, ideas, and encouragement.

CHAPTER 1

Teaching Tips

Learning stations add value to any curriculum, but they are especially valuable to physical education. Learning station popularity in physical education has grown rapidly because stations

- are easily brainstormed and quickly assembled;
- allow students to practice skills both individually and as part of a team;
- increase students' time on task;
- afford physical educators great opportunities to make individualized assessments of student progress;
- open the doors to cross-curricular opportunities with other teachers; and
- are just good, old-fashioned fun.

To make the most of learning through stations, begin by reading and following the suggestions in this chapter. These functional, straightforward tips are simply meant as jumping off points—ideas and suggestions to get you thinking about all of the ways learning stations can add fitness and fun to daily lessons. Once stations have been successfully implemented in the classroom, use these guidelines to build new stations based on new or revised curriculum objectives.

Make It Simple—Finding Your Inspiration

Finding your inspiration is the hardest part to making learning stations an integral and ongoing part of your physical education curriculum. The best way to get started is to do the following: Review your current and past curriculum objectives; ask fellow teachers to share upcoming lesson plans; and look creatively at your monthly calendar.

Review Curriculum

When you're thinking about trying out learning stations, a great place to start is to review your annual curriculum and state guidelines. Consider what you need to achieve, when you need to achieve it by, and which methods you typically use to accomplish your desired curriculum outcomes. Then, sit down with a notepad and pen to write your answers to the following questions:

- When do I usually teach particular curriculum skills? Are they calendar driven or sequential?
- What skills seem consistently challenging to most students?
- How do I assess students on these skills?
- What additional opportunities for guided practice can I provide?
- Are there classroom teachers in my building who are teaching skills or concepts that complement my physical education curriculum?

After you consider the answers to these questions, you will be ready to learn more about how to generate station-based ideas that directly relate to basic curriculum goals and objectives.

Ask Around

The last question in particular provides an opportunity for a wonderful break in the normal teaching routine. Station lessons inspired by other classroom teachers break up the monotony of repeating your lesson plans and at the same time are often invaluable in reinforcing basic concepts and ideas in other core subject areas. So, don't be shy! Informally survey staff and colleagues about what is upcoming in their lesson plans. You might be surprised at how easily stations can be created to bring subject matter to life.

For example, consider starting off station planning with basic curriculum that overlaps into physical education—like the circulatory system. A station like the *Healthy Heart Circuits* station in this book can be set up to help students see the connection between the heart's functions in the body through movement and physical exertion. This station accomplishes not only health or biology learning objectives but also physical education requirements. Of equal importance is the fact that it yields maximum results by accomplishing both of these goals with minimal effort and planning.

Again, to make the most of this cooperation, take a hard look at other subject areas and ask other teachers for their thoughts—even if the curriculum doesn't seem to lend itself to physical education classes at first glance. You might be surprised how easily reading basics, math skills, and social studies trivia can be adapted through creativity and good planning. Just taking an extra bit of thought and ingenuity can make everything—from Earth Day and animal habitats to reading and math—more productive and fun through learning stations.

Check a Calendar

Finally, another great starting point for station inspiration is your monthly calendar. Consider adding a station once a month for an end-of-the-month wrap-up. The additional practice adds confidence to students who might have felt awkward earlier in the month but can now truly enjoy the activity by the end of the month. Using stations at the beginning of a complicated unit can also be effective when planned carefully.

For example, a lesson on dribbling at the beginning of a basketball unit can be reinforced through stations that provide extra skills practice such as dribbling around cones or dribbling around a partner. In fact, each skill needed to successfully complete the basket-ball unit could be broken down into a weekly station activity. The end-of-the-month wrap-up station could find you evaluating students' progress as they move through the stations.

Also, remember to check your calendar for community events, special seasonal observances, or holidays that may provide great chances for learning and fun. Again, since celebrations are usually schoolwide, this is another opportunity to tie physical education skills to learning in other areas. Students love celebrations in the gym that explore learning in nontraditional ways.

Make It Fun–Planning Makes Perfect

Once you decide when and where station lessons fit into your curriculum, it becomes time to decide how you can most effectively incorporate them. While there are many things to consider, what should be at the top of your list are the design, the instructional techniques, and the use of clear expectations.

Design the Lesson

Designing station-based lessons involves outlining your instructional objectives, assessing skill levels, checking equipment and environment, and most of all, using your imagination. The most useful stations are those that build on previously learned skills. So, when designing your station, first consider the upcoming unit you have slotted for a station-based lesson. Outlining the basic skills and concepts the students use throughout the unit is a helpful starting point. This could be as simple as jotting down your mental notes on a piece of scrap paper, or it could be as involved as creating a spreadsheet of to-do items. After determining goals and objectives, target 3 to 10 of these skills as potential stations. Think of the skills in terms of complexity, number of participants, and student value. Make sure that the skills you choose directly relate to the unit outcomes you are trying to achieve.

For example, if one of your unit goals is to focus on teamwork, then you need to make sure that you have at least one teamwork opportunity in your station lesson for children to build on.

Also, remember to consider both the age and skill level of your students. Since station activities are somewhat self-guided, station activities must be age appropriate and easy to follow. Similarly, skill level must be carefully weighed. Students become frustrated if the station is too hard, and they get bored if the station is too easy. Common teaching sense should guide you to strive for a happy medium, adapting any part of the stations to appropriately challenge your students.

In addition to keeping the skill level in mind, make sure your students know the proper techniques and safety precautions essential to each skill. For instance, a first grader who has not been taught a forward roll will not do one correctly and could risk both embarrassment as well as serious injury. In general, keeping the overall objective in mind, weighing the skill level and age range, and knowing the objective of the specific lesson all ensure a successful station.

Decide on Instruction

In the early planning stages, it is important to establish the number of students per station, the sequence of stations, and how and when you want students to transition from activity to activity. There are literally hundreds of ways to divide, sequence, and transition classes for stations.

To divide students, I often divide the class by birthdays, shirt color, or eye color. Occasionally, I have students count off into groups of three to four. But what I really like to do is to empower students by giving them the ultimate choice. First, I spend a few minutes talking to them about making good decisions and cooperating. Then, I ask them to make good decisions and choose their own group. If they choose to accept my challenge, they are responsible for their group's behavior. Not only does this give students the power to choose, it also keeps classroom management to a minimum. I rarely have a problem with tattling or sharing.

Also, when planning instructions for stations, remember to think about the sequence of the stations themselves. Often sequencing is dictated by both the skills and the theme of your station. Maybe you want students to do a station lesson on interval training where they alternate weight-bearing exercise with cardiovascular training. Or maybe, like in the example of the *Healthy Heart Circuits*, students must follow the path that oxygen takes throughout the body on the way to the heart. Again, planning ahead and sketching out a visual roadmap aids in deciding sequencing.

One final consideration in planning stations is transitioning. Transitions are wonderful tools for smoothly moving students from one activity to another. Music is a great tool for transitioning, but so are bells, drums, hand claps, and whistles. The most important aspect of transitions is that the students be given a detailed explanation ahead of time so that they understand your expectations and can execute the procedure well. Usually, after explaining and demonstrating all the stations, I tell the students how and when they move to the next station. I prefer music for most activities. Specifically, I usually use a '50s or '60s greatest hits CD or another CD that adds to the theme of activities. I explain to students that they work at the station while the music is playing and that they stop when the music stops. Many times I include that they need to stop, clean up the station, and sit quietly until the music begins again. I have younger students point to the station they are supposed to go to next. At the transition point, I have their attention and use this time to give additional instructions or make announcements. When the music starts, they then walk to the next station and begin.

Prepare Equipment

Preparing equipment may be as simple as sketching out a floor plan of the gymnasium and spacing equipment evenly. Or, depending on your attention to detail, it may be a roadmap drawn to scale, complete with a legend and a detailed listing of equipment or tools. Regardless of your personal style, sketching out ideas and listing materials and equipment ahead of time definitely make setup and instruction much easier on the day of the lesson.

Before teaching the station lesson, have all of your activities out and set up before your students enter your facility. Each station game has a *Preparation* section that offers suggestions on what to do before your students begin class. Remember, try to set the stations up in an easy or obvious pattern. I usually try to set up around the perimeter of the gym and have one or two stations in the middle. See figure 1.1 for examples of basic station floor plans.

Numbering each station is also helpful and makes transitions easier. This also is a great way to integrate number order in your lower grade-classes. Make the numbers easy to read by labeling cones or putting signs on the wall or numbers on the floor. Station signs (figure 1.2) also help the students remember the activity and can briefly outline that particular station's instructions. In general, I always try to put the number, name of the station, and instructions or a picture on the sign.

A word about the equipment used in these station games. It is a good idea to give yourself at least a couple of weeks to inspect and, if needed, replace or order additional equipment. Check each piece

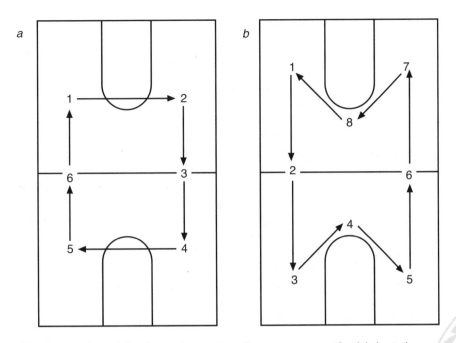

Figure 1.1 Organizing the stations using a floor arrangement for *(a)* six stations or for *(b)* eight stations.

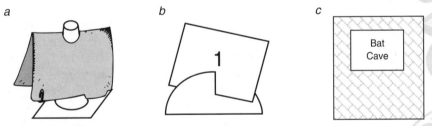

Figure 1.2 Ways to label stations. Use a *(a)* file folder over a cone, *(b)* a sign in a Styrofoam holder, or *(c)* a sign on the wall.

for safety and stability, function, cleanliness, and age appropriateness. This routine inspection ensures the safety of every child and instills proper attention to maintenance and upkeep.

Make It Matter–Expecting the Best

Instructions and objectives are integral components in planning successful stations. Clear, concise instructions and key words help students focus on the skill while objectives accurately define the purpose for learning the skill.

Define Goals and Objectives

To make instructions and objectives clear, I first do a demonstration of each station, focusing on proper form and technique and outlining the objective associated with the skill. I also provide written instructions for students at each station. For younger students, I demonstrate how to take turns and how to help other students in the group.

For example, if the station is an underhand throw activity, I demonstrate and explain the entire activity: "Stand on the line and put the ball in the hand that you write or color with. Does anyone remember the four steps to a good underhand throw? One, stand like a soldier. Two, swing your arm back. Three, step with your opposite foot. Four, swing your arm forward, point to your target, and release the ball." I continue with, "After you have thrown all three balls the same way, walk to the target, get all of the balls, and give them to the next person in line. Then go to the end of the line and wait until it is your turn again. Your goal is to get two out of three balls to hit the target." I do this for *every* station. Occasionally, I have another student demonstrate the skill, such as how to clean up or how to take turns, for example.

Assess With Confidence

When planned and directed well, stations provide wonderful opportunities to observe your students. I learn a great deal about my students by watching them interact in the less structured station environment. I find it amazing how easy it is from this vantage point to recognize who the leaders are, who the followers are, who the bullies are, and so on.

While observing student interaction, I also watch for skill development to determine if student learning has been demonstrated. At this point, I can mentally evaluate if students are ready to move to the next level. To encourage students to strive for greater skill performance, I frequently recognize a student or group that either demonstrates a superb job on the particular skill or exhibits good cooperation and sportsmanship. I turn the spotlight over to them and let them show everyone what they are doing and how they are doing it. On the other hand, there are often times when it is necessary to stop the class to reteach a skill. This is a good opportunity to redemonstrate and remind them of any key words or concepts.

When I need to evaluate students on an individual basis, I set aside one station. At this station I ask each student to demonstrate the skill that I am assessing. I keep my grade book handy to easily record at the same time. The individual attention the assessment station provides is beneficial in administering feedback and prescribing homework or extra practice as needed.

Evaluate Your Hard Work

At the conclusion of each lesson, I take the time to evaluate the station. I try to look at all aspects from instruction and layout to skills and assessment, taking another look at anything that seemed challenging or could have been improved. I keep this summary in a folder with the rest of my planning notes and file it away until the next time I am ready to do this or a similar station. I also try to get feedback on the station's effectiveness if other teachers or subject areas are involved in the lesson.

Now that you know the basics behind fun, safe, and effective station lessons, let's get started!

CHAPTER 2

Basic Skills

Basic skills are the building blocks of all sports and game skills. They include skills such as throwing, kicking, balance, and locomotion. The lessons in this chapter provide additional ways to reinforce these basics. The lessons are intended to be used in kindergarten through second grades; however, they are easily adaptable to higher grade levels and abilities. Whatever age, in these station games, students isolate and build important, fundamental movements in a low-pressure, fun environment.

Directions, Pathways, and Levels

Grades   **Skills**
K-2   Cardiovascular fitness and endurance, coordi-
                      nation and flexibility, fundamental concepts

Get Started

This lesson is best used to reinforce the sometimes confusing concepts of direction, pathways, and levels in younger students. Mastery of these beginning concepts is not only a basic physical education requirement, but it also helps students gain confidence in their ability both on and off the fields or courts.

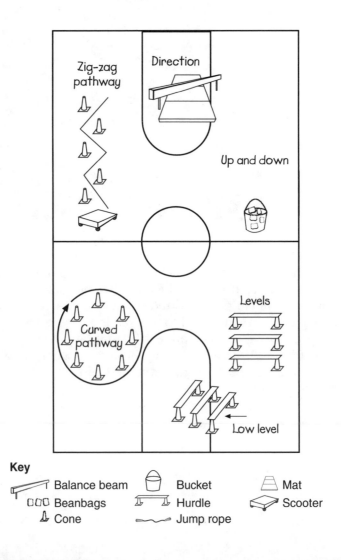

Key

Balance beam	Bucket	Mat
Beanbags	Hurdle	Scooter
Cone	Jump rope	

Zig-Zag Pathway

Equipment Cones (5)
Scooter (1)

Preparation Place the cones in a row, 3 feet from one another.

Objective The student sits on the scooter and zig-zags through the cones without touching any of them.

Direction

Equipment Balance beam (1)
Tumbling mat (1)

Preparation Place the balance beam in the station area away from walls and other equipment. Position the mat underneath the beam.

Objective Students walk forward, backward, and sideways on a balance beam without stopping or touching the ground.

Up and Down

Equipment Beanbags (4-6)
Bowl (or bucket) (1)

Preparation Place the beanbags in the bowl or bucket in the designated station area. Each student gets one beanbag to toss up and catch.

Objective Students catch the beanbag in the bowl three out of five times.

Levels

Equipment Adjustable hurdles (3)

Preparation Place the hurdles in a row about 3 feet from one another.

Objective Students jump over each hurdle using correct form without touching any of them.

Low Level

Equipment Low hurdles (3)

Preparation Place the hurdles about 3 feet from each other.

Objective Students pretend to be snakes and drag themselves under each hurdle.

Curved Pathway

Equipment Cones (4-8)

Preparation Use the cones to create a large circular area.

Objective Students jog around the cones in a curved pathway.

Make It Count
To evaluate the understanding of these concepts, ask students questions during the transition time. Sample questions: "What level does a snake travel in?" "What direction am I walking in?" "Who can show me a zig-zag pathway?"

Make It Safe
Scooters tend to be my students' favorite. Remind them to watch their fingers and not to push one another on the scooters.

Change It Up
How about changing these stations to an obstacle course? Combine several of these stations to create a great obstacle course. Your students not only get a greater understanding of levels, but they also get a cardiovascular workout.

Jumping

Grades
K-2

Skills
Cardiovascular fitness and endurance, coordination and flexibility, fundamental concepts

Get Started
Tie all your jumping skills together with this one lesson. It is guaranteed to give your students a great cardiovascular workout.

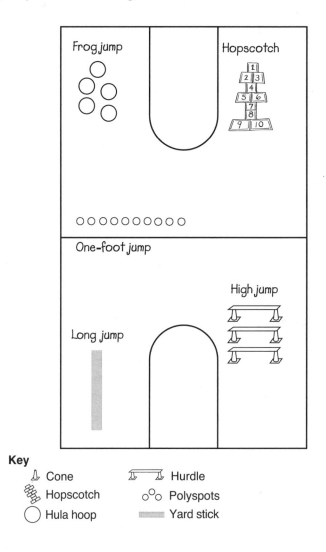

Key

Cone	Hurdle
Hopscotch	Polyspots
Hula hoop	Yard stick

Frog Jump
Equipment Hula hoops (7-10)
Duct tape

Preparation Lay hula hoops on the floor creating lily pads. They may have to be taped down to keep them from moving.

Objective Students jump like a frog from lily pad to lily pad without touching the hula hoop.

Hopscotch
Equipment Hopscotch mat (1)
Duct tape

Preparation Place the hopscotch mat in the designated station area. If mats are not available, tape may be used to create the hopscotch squares. The mat may need to be taped down to prevent it from moving.

Objective Students play hopscotch, staying within the individual squares and jumping on one or both feet.

High Jump
Equipment Low hurdles (3)

Preparation Place the hurdles about 3 feet from each other in the designated station area.

Objective Students take turns jumping over each hurdle using correct form without touching the top.

Long Jump
Equipment Yardstick (1)
Duct tape

Preparation Tape the yardstick to the floor. Place starting line at the beginning of the yardstick.

Objective Students see how far they can jump using correct long-jump form. Specify that they jump with two feet and that they should also land on two feet.

One-Foot Jump
Equipment Polyspots, -stars, or -squares (or circles drawn on the floor) (10-15)

Preparation Place the polyfigures on the floor in a row about 6 inches from one another.

Objective Students attempt to hop on each spot using only one foot.

Make It Count

Take this opportunity to assess your students' jumping skills. I usually stay at one of the centers, evaluating and recording each student's jumping ability as each comes through that station.

Make It Safe

Don't forget to check those tennis shoes. Untied shoes and jumping do not mix. Also, make sure to allow adequate space at the jump rope station to prevent students from getting hit with the ropes.

Change It Up

Your students may enjoy making their own path using the spots at the *One-Foot Jump* station.

Jump Rope Basics

Grades
K-2

Skills
Cardiovascular fitness and endurance, coordination and flexibility, fundamental concepts

Get Started
Does your school participate in Jump Rope for Heart? If so, these stations are a great lead-up lesson.

Individual Rope Jumping

Equipment Jump ropes of appropriate length for the students (5 or 6)

Preparation Lay the ropes in the designated station area.

Objective Students practice the basic bounce, jumping at least five times without stopping.

Long Rope

Equipment Long rope (1)

Preparation Place the rope in an area away from walls and other equipment.

Objective The students in each group take turns turning and jumping the long rope.

Skip-Its

Equipment Skip-its (1 for each student in the group)

Preparation Place the skip-its in the designated station area.

Objective Students successfully use skip-its.

Chinese Jump Rope

Equipment Chinese jump rope (1 for every 3 students in the group)

Preparation Place the Chinese jump ropes in the station area.

Objective Students play previously taught Chinese jump rope games, such as American and the Name Game.

Individual Rope Jumping

Equipment This is a repeat station.

Make It Count

I have stickers made that say "I can jump rope." This lesson is a great opportunity to give out stickers to students who are doing a superb job.

Make It Safe

Be sure all shoestrings are tied. Remind your students that a good jump should be on their toes and should be quiet. I tell my students that there's a difference between jumping and stomping.

Change It Up

This is a good lesson to invite older students to come and help. They can turn the long rope for students and help keep them on task at the other stations.

Locomotor Skills

Grades   **Skills**
K-1   Cardiovascular fitness and endurance, coordination and flexibility, fundamental concepts

Get Started
Here's a different approach to teaching the seven basic locomotor skills.

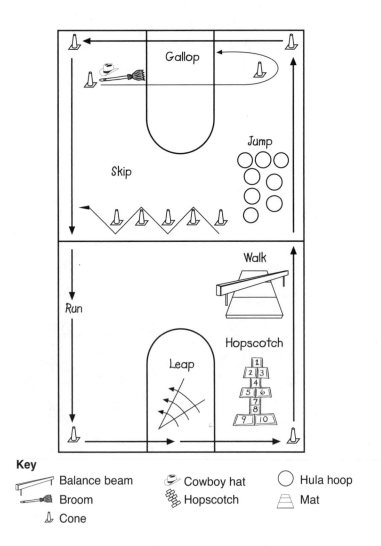

Key
- Balance beam
- Broom
- Cone
- Cowboy hat
- Hopscotch
- Hula hoop
- Mat

Leap

Equipment   Duct tape

Preparation   Apply two long pieces of tape to the floor, creating the sides of a river. You may want to make the river wider at one end and narrower at the other end.

Objective   Students leap across the river.

Skip

Equipment   Cones (5)

Preparation   Place the cones in a line about 3 feet from one another.

Objective   Students demonstrate correct form as they skip through a series of cones.

Gallop

Equipment   Cones (2)
Broomstick (1)
Cowboy hat (1)

Preparation   Place the two cones 15 feet away from each other. Place the broomstick and cowboy hat at the starting cone.

Objective   Students place the broomstick between their legs with the hat on their head and gallop to the other cone and back.

Jump

Equipment   Hula hoops (8-10)

Preparation   Scatter the hula hoops on the floor. They may need to be taped down to prevent them from moving.

Objective   Students jump from hoop to hoop.

Walk

Equipment   Balance beam (1)
Tumbling mats (1 or 2)

Preparation   Place the balance beam in the station area away from walls and other equipment.

Objective   Students walk forward, backward, and sideways on the balance beam without falling off or starting over.

Hopscotch

Equipment   Hopscotch mat (1)
Duct tape

Preparation   Place the hopscotch mat in the designated station area. If mats are not available, tape may be used to create the hopscotch squares. The mat may need to be taped down to prevent it from moving.

Objective   Students play hopscotch, staying within the individual squares and jumping on one or both feet.

Run

Equipment   Cones (4)

Preparation   Arrange the cones into a large square formation, or designate a path around the perimeter of the gym.

Objective   Students jog around the cones for 5 to 10 minutes without walking or stopping.

Make It Count

After teaching these basic movement skills, follow up throughout the year with the other stations in this chapter. Not only is it essential that your students be able to do these skills, but they should also know them by their correct names.

Make It Safe

To provide maximum fun and safety, keep the following in mind: Stress the appropriate way to handle a broomstick; make sure tumbling mats are placed under the balance beam.

Change It Up

These stations lend themselves well to an obstacle course. It would make a great way to close any basic skills lesson.

Balance #1

Grades
K-2

Skills
Coordination and flexibility, fundamental concepts

Get Started
Teaching balance as a part of a gymnastics unit is difficult. This lesson is great because it doesn't include any tumbling or the dreaded *going-upside-down* skill. This pre-gymnastics exercise increases confidence and ensures the balancing skills needed for a successful gymnastics unit.

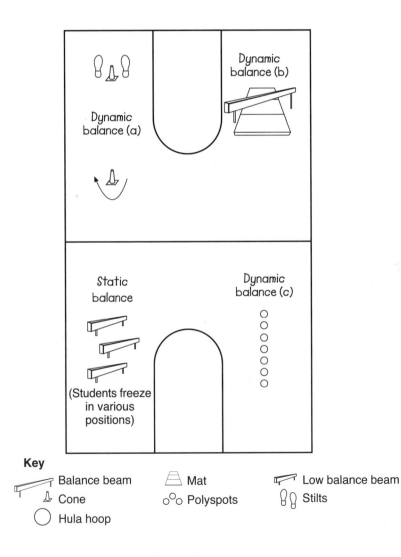

Key

Balance beam	Mat	Low balance beam
Cone	Polyspots	Stilts
Hula hoop		

Dynamic Balance (a)

Equipment   Stilts (1 pair)
Cones (2)

Preparation   Place the cones 5 to 7 feet away from each other, and put the stilts at the starting cone.

Objective   Students take turns using the stilts to walk from one cone to the other and back without stopping or starting over.

Dynamic Balance (b)

Equipment   Balance beam (1)
Tumbling mats (1 or 2)

Preparation   Place the balance beam away from any walls and other equipment. Put tumbling mat under the balance beam.

Objective   Students walk forward, backward, and sideways across a balance beam without falling or starting over.

Dynamic Balance (c)

Equipment   Polyspots, -stars, or -squares (or circles drawn on the floor) (10-12)

Preparation   Arrange the poly-figures in a line about 6 to 8 inches from one another.

Objective   Students take turns stepping on imaginary stones in order to cross an imaginary river without falling in.

Static Balance

Equipment   Low balance beams (2 or 3)
Pictures of various static balances

Preparation   Place the beams 3 to 5 feet from one another in the station area.

Objective   Students perform static balances on the balance beam without using the ground for support.

Make It Count
A review of static and dynamic balances may be necessary before beginning this lesson. To check for understanding, ask your students various balance-related questions about the terms *static* and *dynamic*.

Make It Safe
Be sure to use safety mats wherever you feel it is necessary. Check all equipment (stilts and balance beams) for defects before letting your students use them.

Change It Up
Use soft background music to help set the mood for balancing activities. I usually require the older students to hold their balances longer than the kindergartners.

Balance #2

Grades
2-4

Skills
Coordination and flexibility, fundamental concepts

Get Started

This station builds on those exercises and concepts in *Balance #1*. The skills are reinforced through fun and imaginative activities that all of my kids love!

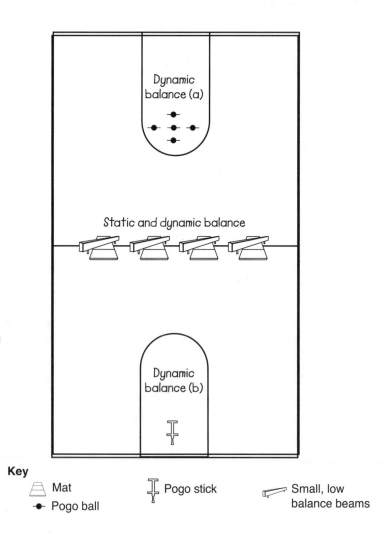

Dynamic balance (a)

Static and dynamic balance

Dynamic balance (b)

Key

△ Mat

T Pogo stick

⟋ Small, low balance beams

•— Pogo ball

Dynamic Balance (a)

Equipment   Pogo ball (1 for each student in the group)

Preparation   Place the pogo balls in the designated station area.

Objective   Students bounce on a pogo ball three to five times consecutively.

Dynamic Balance (b)

Equipment   Pogo stick (1)

Preparation   Place the pogo stick in the station area.

Objective   Students jump 10 consecutive times on the pogo stick.

Static and Dynamic Balance

Equipment   Low balance beams (3-5)
Tumbling mats (1 or 2)

Preparation   Place the balance beams in the station area with mats underneath. Make sure beams are away from walls and other equipment.

Objective   Using their own balance beam, students move to the center of the balance beam and then pose like a statue for a count of 10.

Make It Count

This lesson is most effective if it follows a brief lesson on the difference between static and dynamic balance.

Make It Safe

Using pogo sticks and pogo balls can be a lot of fun for your students. Remind students to follow your safety rules.

Change It Up

Encourage your children to express their creativity when posing like statues.

Ball-Handling Skills

Grades
K-3

Skills
Fundamental concepts, sports skills, teamwork and cooperation

Getting Started
Use this lesson to practice the basic ball-handling skills needed in many sports. I like to use this lesson as a reminder that whatever the sport, a ball only does what you ask it to do.

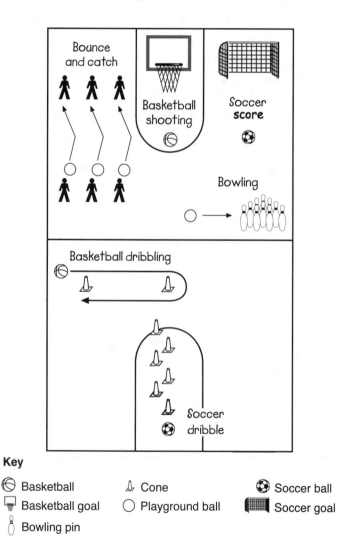

Key

Basketball	Cone	Soccer ball
Basketball goal	Playground ball	Soccer goal
Bowling pin		

Bounce and Catch

Equipment   Playground balls (1 for every 2 students in the group)

Duct tape

Preparation   Place the balls in the station area. It may be necessary to put tape marks on the floor, about 5 to 7 feet apart, for the students to stand on.

Objective   Students bounce and catch a playground ball with a partner.

Basketball Shooting

Equipment   Basketball (1 for each student in the group)

Preparation   Place the basketballs in the basket near the basketball goal.

Objective   Students use correct shooting technique while shooting at the basketball goal.

Soccer Score

Equipment   Soccer ball (1)
Soccer goal (1)
Duct tape

Preparation   Place the goal against a wall.

Apply a tape line to the floor about 10 feet in front of the goal, and place the ball on the line.

Objective   Students attempt to kick the soccer ball into the goal using correct form three out of five times.

Bowling

Equipment   Plastic bowling pins (6-10)
Playground ball (1)
Duct tape

Preparation   Arrange the bowling pins in a triangle formation and place the ball on the tape mark 10 to 12 feet away.

Objective   Students roll the playground ball at the bowling pins, trying to knock them all down.

Soccer Dribble

Equipment   Soccer ball (1)
Cones (2)

Preparation   Place the two cones 10 to 12 feet apart, and place
the soccer ball at the starting cone.

Objective   Students dribble a soccer ball from one cone to
the other and back.

Basketball Dribbling

Equipment   Basketball (1)
Cones (2)

Preparation   Place the cones 7 to 10 feet apart and place the
basketball at the starting cone. A distance of 7 to
10 feet is good for K-2, but the cones can be
farther apart for older students.

Objective   Students dribble a basketball from one cone to
another and back.

Make It Count

This is a great opportunity to assess various skills. Can they dribble
a soccer ball with control? Can they catch a bounced ball or roll a ball
smoothly? Choose the skill you need to evaluate, and station yourself
at that activity. As each group rotates to that station, take the opportunity to watch and record their abilities.

Make It Safe

There is a station in this lesson that requires students to work with
partners. Stress how important it is to pass the ball to the partner. I tell
them, "It isn't fun to play if you always have to chase the ball."

Change It Up

As your students' skill levels improve, set challenges for them to
achieve. For example, keep track of all the correctly performed skills.
Students can also work in pairs and check each other.

Throwing and Tossing

Grades
K-2

Skills
Fundamental concepts, sports skills, teamwork and cooperation

Get Started
This lesson provides numerous opportunities for young students to perfect their underhand throws.

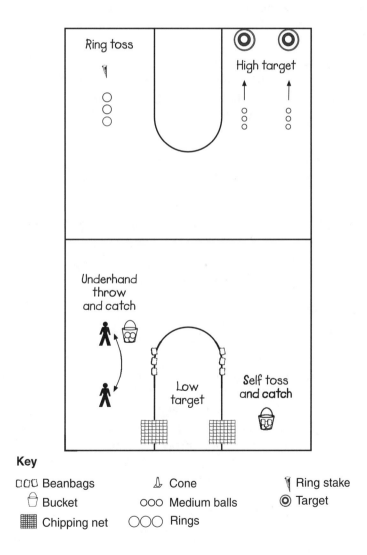

Key

⊡⊡⊡ Beanbags	⚲ Cone	⚑ Ring stake
⊖ Bucket	ооо Medium balls	◎ Target
▦ Chipping net	ОOО Rings	

Low Target
Equipment   Chipping nets or laundry baskets (2)
              Beanbags (3)
              Duct tape

Preparation Place the nets or baskets 5 to 7 feet away from a
              tape line on the floor. Lay the beanbags at the line.

Objective   Students stand on the line and throw each of the
              beanbags at a low target.

Underhand Throw and Catch
Equipment   Foam balls (1 for every 2 students in the group)
              Bowl or bucket (1)

Preparation Have students choose a partner then stand 7 feet
              from each other to toss and catch the foam ball.

Objective   Students demonstrate a correct underhand throw
              by tossing the foam ball back and forth to a
              partner.

Ring Toss
Equipment   Ring toss (1)
              Rings (3)
              Duct tape

Preparation Place the ring toss 5 feet from the tape line on the
              floor. Place the rings on the tape line.

Objective   Students stand at the line and toss each ring,
              making two of three tosses.

High Target
Equipment   Target (hung from wall) (1-2)
              Foam balls (3-6)
              Duct tape

Preparation Hang the target on the wall with the tape. Place a
              tape line on the floor 7 feet from the wall, and lay
              the balls on the line.

Objective   Students stand on the tape line and use an
              underhand throw to throw each ball at the target,
              hitting the target two out of three times.

Self Toss and Catch

Equipment   Beanbags (1 for each person in the group)
Bowl (or bucket) (1)

Preparation   Place the beanbags in a bowl or bucket.

Objective   Students toss and catch a self-thrown beanbag
three out of five times.

Make It Count

Your students are throwing many, many balls during this lesson.
Stress correct form on every throw.

Make It Safe

Be prepared for balls, beanbags, and Wiffle balls to go everywhere; it
is the nature of the activity. Warn your students ahead of time to
watch where they walk and to watch for balls in the air.

Change It Up

Obviously, skill levels can vary a lot between kindergarten and
second grade. To challenge your older students, establish a scoring
system and let them keep score throughout the stations. The throwing distances can be extended and the target sizes can be reduced to
increase the difficulty. To evaluate your students' abilities, pick one
station to stay at. As each group rotates through that station, observe
and record each student's skill level.

Volleying and Striking

Grades	Skills
K-2	Fundamental concepts, sports skills, teamwork and cooperation

Get Started

Striking and volleying can be done with a variety of equipment. This lesson introduces your students to different ways to volley and strike.

Keep It Up

Equipment   Balloons (1 for each person in the group) or beach balls

Preparation   Place the balloons in the designated station area.

Objective   Students strike the balloon upward with a hand or any other body part, trying to keep the balloon from hitting the ground.

Batter Up

Equipment   Batter's tee (1)
Plastic bat (1)
Wiffle or Nerf balls (3)

Preparation   Place the tee 10 feet from a wall. Place the balls and bat near the tee. Have students hit the ball towards the wall.

Objective   Students hit the ball off the tee using the bat correctly two out of three times.

Putt-Putt

Equipment   Putting green (1)
Golf ball (1)
Golf club (1)

Preparation   Roll out the putting green and place the ball and club at one end of the green.

Objective   Students strike the ball gently on the green. If the green has a hole in it to resemble a hole on a golf course, students can then gently strike the ball as close to the hole as possible.

Tennis

Equipment Tennis racket (1)
Tennis ball (1)
Duct tape

Preparation Place a tape line on the floor 8 feet from the wall.
Place the ball and racket near the line.

Objective Students take turns using the racket to volley the
tennis ball against the wall three times.

Score

Equipment Hockey goal (1)
Hockey stick (1)
Puck (1)
Duct tape

Preparation Place the goal up against a wall. Put a tape line on
the floor 10 feet from the goal. Lay the stick and
puck on the tape line.

Objective Students take turns striking the puck with a
hockey stick.

Make It Count

Introduce your students to the different pieces of equipment and
show them how to hold each one. Set goals for the number of times
the students should try to volley the beach ball and balloons. More
advanced students may be able to volley the beach ball back and
forth.

Make It Safe

Using long-handled equipment requires a few extra safety rules. I do
not allow my students to swing the golf clubs, hockey sticks, bats, or
tennis rackets. I also require that the students who are waiting for
their turns stand back, about 3 to 4 feet away. I usually have to lay
something on the floor to mark this spot.

Change It Up

If you have not introduced one or two of these pieces of equipment,
or if you do not want your kindergartners using golf clubs or bats,
replace it with a cardiovascular activity.

Variety

Grades
K-2

Skills
Cardiovascular fitness and endurance, coordination and flexibility, fundamental concepts

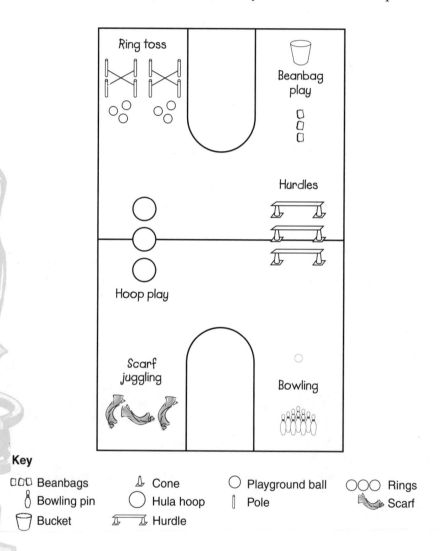

Key

☐☐☐ Beanbags	⚲ Cone	○ Playground ball	○○○ Rings
⚱ Bowling pin	○ Hula hoop	▯ Pole	〰 Scarf
⛩ Bucket	⚏ Hurdle		

Hoop Play

Equipment Hula hoops (1 for each student in the group)

Preparation Place the hula hoops in the designated station area

Objective Students attempt to hula hoop using various parts of their body.

Ring Toss

Equipment Ring toss (1-2)
Rings (3-6)

Preparation Place the ring-toss target in the station area, and place the rings 5 feet away on a tape line.

Objective Students toss each ring at the target making two out of three tosses.

Beanbag Play

Equipment Beanbags (3)
Bucket (or another type of beanbag target) (1)
Duct tape

Preparation Place the target in the designated station area. Apply a tape line to the floor about 7 feet from the target, and lay the beanbags at the line.

Objective Students use an underhand throw to toss each beanbag into the bucket or at the target.

Hurdles

Equipment Adjustable hurdles (2 or 3)

Preparation Place the hurdles in a row, about 3 feet from one another.

Objective Students take turns jumping and leaping over each of the hurdles without touching them.

Bowling

Equipment Plastic bowling pins (6-10)
Playground ball (1)
Duct tape

Preparation Place the bowling pins in a triangle. Apply the tape line to the floor about 8 to 10 feet from the pins. Position the ball at the line.

Objective Students roll a playground ball at the bowling pins, knocking over as many as possible.

Scarf Juggling

Equipment   Scarves (2 or 3 per child in the group)

Preparation   Place all of the scarves in the designated station area.

Objective   Students explore different ways of tossing and catching two or three scarves as a juggler using balls would.

Make It Count

I often use this lesson when a substitute is going to be there. It uses a lot of equipment but is relatively simple to set up. The skills are basic, and most substitutes can judge whether they are being done correctly.

Make It Safe

This lesson involves a lot of moving objects. I always emphasize to the students the importance of being aware of what is going on around them at all times.

Change It Up

Substitute any station for activities your students love to do. I usually include Chinese jump rope because my students love to do it. Don't forget to play fun, upbeat music.

Sports Fundamentals

The lessons in this chapter are designed primarily for third grade through sixth grade. The emphasis is on developing those skills necessary for active participation in various sports. The stations are excellent for practicing skills without heading blindly into an entire game situation. Although many students participate in sports outside of school, the students who do not have this opportunity enjoy participating in this low-pressure, noncompetitive environment. A great addition to these lessons is to provide instruction in developing lifetime sports or hobbies, such as tennis and golf.

Gymnastics

Grades
3-6

Skills
Coordination and flexibility, fundamental concepts, sports skills

Get Started

Tumbling skills can be difficult to teach, so many of the skills require hands-on teaching and spotting. These stations are lead-up skills that can be done independently. This independent work allows the teacher to stay at one station and give individual instruction and spotting.

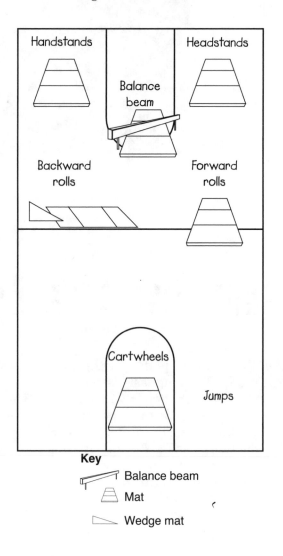

Handstands

Headstands

Balance beam

Backward rolls

Forward rolls

Cartwheels

Jumps

Key

Balance beam

Mat

Wedge mat

Forward Rolls

Equipment Tumbling mats (1 or 2)

Preparation Position the tumbling mats in a safe area away from walls and other equipment.

Objective Students perform a correct forward roll on the tumbling mat. Students should start and finish in the standing position.

Jumps

Equipment Poster or pictures of each of the various jumps—pike, straddle, tuck, half turn, full turn

Preparation Hang the pictures on the wall in the station area.

Objective Students demonstrate correct form when jumping.

Cartwheels

Equipment Tumbling mat (1)

Preparation Position the mat in the station area. It may be necessary to draw hand and feet prints to indicate how to start and finish.

Objective Students perform cartwheels on a tumbling mat using correct form three out of five times.

Backward Rolls

Equipment Wedge mat (1)
Tumbling mat (1)

Preparation Place the tumbling mat at the bottom of the wedge mat.

Objective Students practice backward rolls using correct form and technique.

Handstands

Equipment Tumbling mat (1)

Preparation Place the tumbling mat in an area away from walls and other equipment. Make sure only one student is on the mat at a time.

Objective Students perform handstands on a tumbling mat.

Balance Beam

Equipment   Balance beam (1)
Tumbling mats (1 or 2)

Preparation   Place the balance beam away from other equipment. Place the mats under the equipment.

Objective   Students use various locomotor skills to travel
across the balance beam without falling or
starting over.

Headstands

Equipment   Tumbling mat (1)

Preparation   Place the tumbling mat in an area away from walls
and other equipment. It may be helpful to draw
marks on the mat to indicate where hands and
head should be positioned.

Objective   Students practice headstands on a tumbling mat,
successfully holding position for 30 seconds.

Make It Count
Decide which skill you want to focus on during this lesson. I recom-
mend that the teacher stay at that station to either evaluate the
students or give additional help and spotting.

Make It Safe
Proper form and technique are essential in preventing injuries. Stress
the importance of following instructions, taking turns, and not
playing on the equipment.

Change It Up
Skills such as dive forward rolls, round-offs, or skill routines also can
be substituted or added to the stations. For classes with lower skills,
substitute stations with fitness activities, such as sit-ups, pull-ups,
jogging, and so on.

Softball

Grades   **Skills**
3-6   Sports skills, teamwork and cooperation

Get Started
This is a great lesson to do before playing an actual game of softball. As we all know, not all students are highly skilled. Stations like this allow every student a personalized activity. The higher skilled students can continue to improve their skills and the other students can continue to develop skills without actually playing the game.

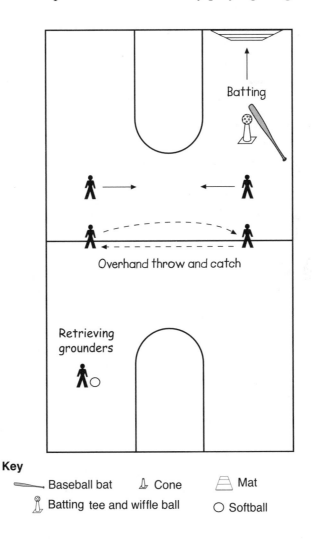

Key

Baseball bat   Cone   Mat

Batting tee and wiffle ball   Softball

Retrieving Grounders

Equipment   Softball (or rubber ball) (1)

Preparation   Have students stand 12 feet from a wall and throw the ball toward the lower half of the wall and retrieve the returning ball.

Objective   Students throw the ball and retrieve the grounder 3 to 5 times.

Batting

Equipment   Batting tee (1)
Wiffle ball (1)
Bat (1)

Preparation   Place the tee 12 feet from a wall. Lay the wiffle ball and bat beside the tee. Have students hit the ball off the tee toward the wall.

Objective   Students take turns striking the ball off a tee using the correct stance and flat swing.

Overhand Throw and Catch

Equipment   Rag softballs (1 for every 2 students in the group)

Preparation   Have students stand 15 to 20 feet from their partners and throw the ball using an overhand throw.

Objective   Students throw and catch a rag ball or softball with a partner using correct form.

Make It Count

For your students to get the most out of this lesson, they need to practice the skills correctly. It is very important to review each skill and any key words or concepts before beginning the lesson.

Make It Safe

It is always to good idea to point out potentially hazardous areas. For example, the batting area can be trouble. Have students who are waiting to bat stand behind a line a safe distance away. Remind the batter that throwing the bat is not necessary. Also, a lot of balls are moving throughout the gym at the same time. All students need to be watching for balls as well as trying to keep their balls in their area.

Change It Up

To challenge your higher level students, set higher standards for them. Make any targets smaller, and require them to throw and catch without dropping the ball.

Basketball

Grades
3-6

Skills
Sports skills, teamwork and cooperation

Get Started
This lesson requires using a gymnasium with two basketball goals. An oversized gym would be an added bonus. Once again, using these stations helps the lower skilled students improve their skills in a noncompetitive environment, and the higher skilled students can still perfect their skills.

Key

🏀 Basketball

🏀 Basketball goal

⌒ Cone

Basketball Dribbling

Equipment   Basketball (1)
Cones (5)

Preparation   Place the cones in a straight line, spaced about 3 feet from one another. Place the basketball at the starting cone.

Objective   Students dribble a basketball through cones using the left hand, the right, then both hands.

Lay-Ups

Equipment   Basketball goal (1)
Basketball (1)

Preparation   Have students take turns practicing lay-ups.

Objective   Students make at least 7 out of 10 lay-ups.

Free Throw Shots

Equipment   Basketball (1)
Basketball goal (1)

Preparation   Have students stand at the free throw line or a line of tape marking the correct distance from the goal. Students shoot each ball and then retrieve them for the next student.

Objective   Students make 5 out of 10 free throw shots.

Basketball Passes

Equipment   Basketball (1)

Preparation   Have students first form a circle, then use one of the following to pass the ball to someone else in the group: chest pass, overhead pass, and bounce pass.

Objective   Students pass the basketball with proper form using the bounce, chest, and overhead passes.

Make It Count

As the teacher, you should constantly monitor all of the activities. Require that all students do each of the skills correctly with proper form.

Make It Safe

To cut down on the number of balls out in the gym, try to put only one ball at each of the stations.

Change It Up

If your gym is set up to allow it, have a small group playing basketball at one end of the gym, and set the stations up at the other end. This allows higher skilled students to work on strategies and the others to work on skills. If the class is large, add a few fitness stations.

Volleyball #1

Grades
3-6

Skills
Sports skills, teamwork and cooperation

Get Started

Volleyball is becoming a more popular sport in our area. The junior high school has recently started a girls' volleyball team, and I have noticed an increased interest in the sport. The request from the junior high coaches was that the students be able to do the basic skills correctly. The following station works mainly on those basic skills.

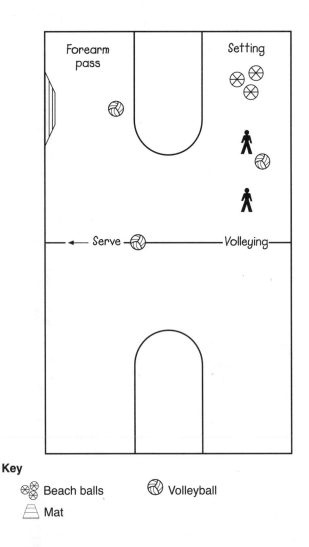

Key

⊗⊗ Beach balls   ⊘ Volleyball
△ Mat

Forearm Pass

Equipment   Volleyball trainer (1) or mat

Preparation   Have students stand 5 to 7 feet from the wall with the ball.

Objective   Students volley the ball to the wall using a forearm pass.

Setting

Equipment   Inflated beach balls (1 for each student in the group)

Preparation   Place the beach balls in the station area.

Objective   Students attempt to set the beach ball three times in a row.

Volleying

Equipment   Volleyball (1 for every 2 students in the group)

Preparation   Have pairs of students stand 10 feet apart and volley the ball back and forth.

Objective   Students pass the ball back and forth three to five consecutive times.

Serve

Equipment   Duct tape
Volleyball (1)

Preparation   Apply a piece of tape to the wall at the height of a volleyball net. Place another piece of tape on the floor the appropriate length away from the wall. Have the student stand at the tape line.

Objective   Students stand at the tape line and serve the volleyball toward the wall, trying to hit the wall above the tape line.

Make It Count

Hand position is a controversial issue. There are several methods in vogue. Find the one that is supported by the local coaches and use that in your lessons.

Make It Safe

Emphasize the importance of using correct form and hand position to minimize injuries to fingers and hands.

Change It Up

It may be necessary to add stations to round out the activities; consider a fitness station. Kids these days can never get enough sit-ups and pull-ups.

Volleyball #2

Grades   **Skills**
3-6   Sports skills, teamwork and cooperation

Get Started
A gymnasium is the best location to do this lesson. A gym with extra room on the side is an added benefit.

Key
 Large net
Small, low net
Volleyball

Volleying

Equipment   Small, low nets (2)
Standards (4)
Volleyballs (2)

Preparation   Arrange the two nets on the other side of the gym. Divide the remaining students among the two nets and have them practice using forearm pass to keep the volleyball going across the net.

Objective   Students practice volleying across the low nets using correct form and without hitting the net.

Volleyball Game

Equipment   Large volleyball net (1)
Standards (2)
Volleyball (1)
Duct tape

Preparation   Set the volleyball net up on half of the gym floor. Use tape to mark the boundary lines. Have two groups of students play against each other. Show the students how to rotate and keep score.

Objective   Students participate in a volleyball game and learn the rules of volleyball.

Make It Count

Use the mini volleyball game to review rules, scoring, and basic strategy.

Make It Safe

Remind your students that they must "call the ball" if they are going to hit it. This prevents two students from running into each other.

Change It Up

If your students have already learned to play volleyball, use this time to call students over one at a time to evaluate skills or do fitness testing.

Soccer #1

Grades   **Skills**
K-3   Sports skills, teamwork and cooperation

Get Started
Soccer is a continually growing pastime for both younger and older students. Outlining the right form and the importance of playing by the rules at a young age ensures that the enjoyment and safety of the sport continue.

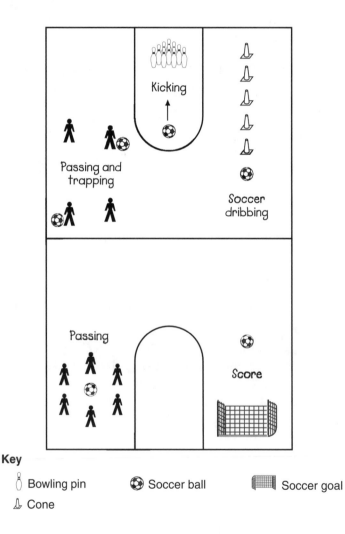

Key

  Bowling pin   Soccer ball   Soccer goal

  Cone

Soccer Dribbling

Equipment   Soccer ball (1)
Cones (5)

Preparation   Place the cones in a line about 3 feet from one another. Place the ball at the beginning cone.

Objective   Students dribble a soccer ball through cones using correct form and without bumping the cones.

Score

Equipment   Portable soccer goal (1)
Soccer ball (1)
Duct tape

Preparation   Set the soccer goal up against a wall and place a tape line on the floor 7 to 10 feet.

Objective   Students kick a soccer ball into a goal using correct form three out of five times.

Passing

Equipment   Soccer ball (1)

Preparation   Have students in the group stand and form a circle, passing the ball around the circle.

Objective   Students pass the soccer ball around the circle using correct form.

Passing and Trapping

Equipment   Soccer balls (1 for every 2 students in the group)

Preparation   Have students stand 10 to 12 feet from a partner and have them pass the soccer ball to each other with control and proper form. Have each partner trap the ball before passing it back.

Objective   Students accurately pass and trap a soccer ball with a partner 7 out of 10 times.

Kicking

Equipment   Soccer ball (1)
Plastic bowling pins (or two-liter bottles) (10)

Preparation   Place the bowling pins in a triangle. Place a tape line on the floor 10 to 12 feet away from the pins. Have students stand at the tape line.

Objective   Students kick a soccer ball to knock down the bowling pins.

Make It Count

Stop your students occasionally to point out who is demonstrating great soccer skills.

Make It Safe

Remind your students that they need to be aware of things going on around them at all times. Sometimes my students can get carried away at the *Kicking* station. To prevent injuries and mishaps, I do not allow a goalie, and the students must retrieve their own soccer balls.

Change It Up

To add difficulty, attach a poster to the wall at each station with a goal to meet. For example, a **gold level** student can pass a soccer ball with a partner five times without missing. A **silver level** student can pass a soccer ball with a partner three times without missing. A **bronze level** student can pass a soccer ball with a partner two times without missing.

Soccer #2

Grades   **Skills**
3-6   Sports skills, teamwork and cooperation

Get Started
This lesson is slightly more advanced than the other one. These stations tend to target specialized skills that older students enjoy practicing.

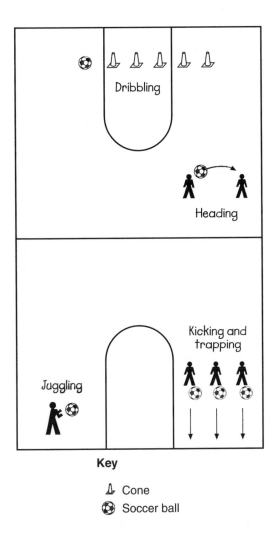

Key

🔸 Cone
⚽ Soccer ball

Kicking and Trapping

Equipment   Soccer balls (1 for each student in the group)

Preparation   Have students stand 10 to 15 feet from the wall with their soccer ball.

Objective   Students kick a ball towards the wall and trap the returning ball. This doesn't require a partner.

Juggling

Equipment   Soccer balls (1 for each student in the group)

Preparation   Give each student his own ball and a designated area.

Objective   Each student has a ball to practice juggling using their knees and feet.

Dribbling

Equipment   Soccer ball (1)
Cones (5)

Preparation   Set the cones out in a line about 3 feet from one another. Place the ball at the beginning cone.

Objective   Each student dribbles the ball through the cones and back demonstrating correct form and skill.

Heading

Equipment   Soccer balls (1 for every 2 students in the group)

Preparation   Have students stand 10 to 12 feet from a partner. Have each student take turns tossing the ball so that the other person can head it.

Objective   Students successfully head a tossed ball three out of five times.

Make It Count

Because these skills are more advanced, monitor your students closely. My students tend to lose focus quickly when they are not successful at an activity.

Make It Safe

It is a good idea to use both real and Nerf soccer balls at the heading and juggling stations. This allows beginners the option of using the softer balls.

Change It Up

You can make this lesson more challenging by increasing the goal at each station. Require higher skilled students to increase the number of times they juggle the ball, or increase the speed at which they dribble through the cones.

Hockey

Grades   **Skills**
3-6   Sports skills, teamwork and cooperation

Get Started
Hockey has become quite popular in our area. Students love to pretend to be a star hockey player winning a big game. Use these stations to help them improve their skills.

Key
Bowling pin
Cone
Hockey puck/stick

Puck Handling
Equipment Puck (1)
Cones (5)
Hockey stick (1)

Preparation Place the cones in a line about 3 feet apart from one another. Set the hockey stick and puck at the starting cone.

Objective Students move the puck using the hockey stick through cones and back to the beginning cone.

Puck Passing
Equipment Hockey stick (1 for each student in the group)
Puck (1 for every 2 students in the group)

Preparation Give each student a hockey stick and then have them get into pairs. Have students stand 10 to 15 feet apart to pass the puck back and forth using a correct hockey pass.

Objective Students accurately pass a puck to their partner 5 out of 7 times.

Hot Potato
Equipment Puck (1)
Hockey sticks (1 for each student in the group)

Preparation Give each student a hockey stick and have the students arrange themselves into a large circle.

Objective Students pass the puck to another person in the circle 5 out of 7 times with completed and accurate passes.

Shooting
Equipment Pucks (3)
Hockey stick (1)
Bowling pins (6-10)

Preparation Set the pins upright in a triangle formation. Tape a line on the floor 10 to 12 feet in front of the bowling pins. Place the puck and hockey stick at the line.

Objective Students take turns shooting each puck at bowling pins.

Make It Count

To make each station more challenging, establish a goal to accomplish. Group the students according to ability level to allow them to compete with each other.

Make It Safe

The thought of all those hockey sticks in my students' hands is enough to send chills down my spine. To prevent injuries and accidents, I have found these guidelines work pretty well: The hockey stick never goes any higher than knee level, and a penalty box does exist in my gym. Students who have difficulty controlling their stick spend a little time in my penalty box.

Change It Up

Add fitness activities, or do individual skill evaluations during this lesson.

Tennis

Grades
3-6

Skills
Sports skills, teamwork and cooperation

Get Started

First, it can be done. Spread your students out all around the gym, and expect balls to go everywhere. It is okay.

Forehand Stroke

Equipment Tennis rackets (2)
Tennis balls (2)

Preparation Place the rackets about 10 to 12 feet from the wall. Be sure to allow plenty of space for two students to work at the same time.

Objective Two students stand away from the wall and use only a forehand stroke to hit the ball against the wall 5 to 10 times.

Backhand Stroke

Equipment Tennis rackets (2)
Tennis balls (2)

Preparation Place the rackets 10 to 15 feet from the wall.

Objective Two students at a time use the backhand stroke to hit the ball against the wall 5 to 10 times.

Ball Bounce

Equipment Tennis racket (1)
Tennis balls (1 for each student in the group)

Preparation Lay a ball on each racket in the designated station area.

Objective Each student bounces a tennis ball on the face of the tennis racket 10 to 20 times.

Volley

Equipment Tennis net (1)
Standards (2)
Rackets (2-4)

Preparation Set the net up in the center of the gym. Make sure to leave a lot of room around the perimeter of the court.

Objective Two to four students volley the tennis ball across the net.

Make It Count
Watch for students who are doing the skills correctly. Let them demonstrate for the others.

Make It Safe
Remind your students to watch for tennis balls on the floor so that they don't trip.

Change It Up
If this lesson has too many tennis stations for your gym, replace a few with fitness activities. Then do the others another day.

CHAPTER 4

Fitness Essentials

As the fitness level of our nation's children continues to drop, we, as physical educators, are beginning to feel the pressure to incorporate basic fitness concepts and activities into our curriculum. Unfortunately, physical education class may be the only time some students get a physical workout. The lessons in this chapter address those basic concepts of cardiovascular and muscular endurance and muscle identification—all of which are necessary in maintaining lifelong fitness.

Muscle Building

Grades
3-6

Skills
Cross-curricular study, strength training and conditioning

Get Started
Learning anatomy is difficult. Give your students a head start. As you teach your students about fitness, introduce the various muscles using their correct names. Students can then learn their muscles as they work out.

Key

🪑 Chair   ⌣ Jump rope   ⇒ Step box
⊓ Chin-up bar   △ Mat

Biceps

Equipment Chin-up bars (1 or 2)
Tumbling mat (1)

Preparation Place the tumbling mat on the floor under the chin-up bar.

Objective Students take turns doing pull-ups or flex-arm hangs from a chin-up bar.

Abdominals

Equipment Tumbling mat (1)

Preparation Place the mat in the designated station area.

Objective Students perform a designated number of sit-ups, crunches, knee-to-chest twists, or curl-ups on a tumbling mat.

Triceps

Equipment Tumbling mat (1)
Standard four-legged chair with no wheels (1)

Preparation Place the mat in the designated area and position the chair off to the side.

Have students alternate between doing push-ups on the mat and chair-dips on the chair.

Objective Students perform 10 push-ups on the mat and 10 chair-dips on the chair.

Hamstrings

Equipment Duct tape

Preparation Place two tape lines on the floor 20 feet from each other.

Objective Students perform lunge steps from one tape line to the other.

Calves

Equipment Step boxes (optional) (4 or 5)

Preparation Place the steps on the floor against a wall. If steps are not available, just make sure the station is located at a wall.

Have students stand on the steps facing the wall with their heels off the edge. Instruct them to flex then relax their heels.

Objective Students perform a designated number of heel raises.

Cardiovascular

Equipment   Jump ropes (1 for each student in the group)

Preparation   Place the jump ropes in the designated station area.

Objective   Students jump rope a predetermined number of times.

Make It Count

I like to provide a picture of the appropriate muscle and its name at each station. The younger students enjoy labeling a large poster of a body. During the transition time, ask appropriate questions concerning the muscles.

Make It Safe

Before beginning any strenuous workout, make the students stretch out. Constantly reinforce correct form at each station.

Change It Up

Your older students may enjoy working with a partner and taking turns at each exercise station. They may also need a set number of repetitions to complete at each station. Do not hesitate to change any of the stations to a more familiar activity.

Resistance Training

Grades   **Skills**
3-6   Strength training and conditioning

Get Started
Tired of the same old calisthenics? Try resistance bands. They are
easy to use and very inexpensive. Resistance bands are wide strips of
stretchable rubber—almost like giant rubber bands. Your students
will love them.

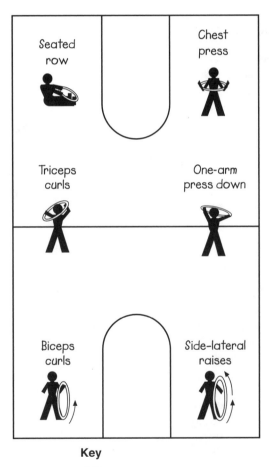

Key

⬭ Resistance band

Seated Row
Equipment   1 one-yard strip of resistance band for each student in the group

Preparation   Have the students sit on the floor in pike positions and place center of band across the soles of both feet. Have students begin by grasping the ends of the band with palms inward and elbows close to body. Then instruct students to sit up tall with chest lifted. Have students slowly bring the hands toward the body, then squeeze the shoulder blades together—pause—and slowly return to the starting position.

Objective   Students perform 15 seated rows.

Chest Press
Equipment   1 one-yard strip of resistance band for each student in the group

Preparation   While students are standing with feet shoulder-width apart, have them place the center of the resistance band across their back and under their arms. Then have them grip the band ends with both hands in front of each underarm and take up the slack until the band rests snugly against the back. Have them push arms forward and slowly return to starting position.

Objective   Students successfully perform 15 chest presses.

One-Arm Press Down
Equipment   1 one-yard strip of resistance band for each student in the group

Preparation   Have students grasp both ends of the band while standing upright so the length of the band is shoulder-width apart. Have students extend their left arm overhead and their right hand out to the side. Then instruct them to pull their right elbow out and down toward body, keeping wrists straight—pause—and slowly return to starting position. Have the students repeat using the other arm.

Objective   Students successfully perform 15 one-arm press downs with each arm.

Side-Lateral Raises

Equipment   1 one-yard strip of resistance band for each student in the group.

Preparation   Have students place one end of the band under their right foot while standing upright with feet shoulder-width apart. Next, have them grasp the other end of the band with their right hand. Instruct them to slowly raise arm upward and out from the side of the body until arm is just below shoulder height—pause—then slowly return to starting position. Have them repeat using the other arm.

Objective   Students successfully perform 15 side-lateral raises on each arm.

Biceps Curls

Equipment   1 one-yard strip of resistance band for each student in the group

Preparation   Instruct students to place one end of the band under their right foot while they are standing upright with feet shoulder-width apart. Next, have them grip the other end of the band with their right hand at a point where the slack is taken up. Then have them place the elbow close to the body, palm facing upward, and instruct them to slowly curl forearm upward toward the shoulder—pause—and slowly return to starting position.

Objective   Students perform 15 biceps curls with each arm.

Triceps Curls

Equipment   1 one-yard strips of resistance band for each student in the group

Preparation   Have students first place one end of the band in their right hand, then put their left hand behind their back, grasping the band at that point while they are standing upright with their feet shoulder-width apart. Next, have them slowly straighten their right arm toward the ceiling—pause—then slowly return to the starting position.

Objective   Students perform 15 triceps curls with each arm.

Make It Count

These exercises are beneficial only when done correctly. Be sure to walk around and watch your students while they are at each station.

Make It Safe

As mentioned earlier, the resistance bands are large rubber bands. In the hands of young people, they can be quite dangerous. I am extremely strict about how my students handle resistance bands. The consequences for misuse are usually severe. Be sure to set the guidelines before they begin.

Change It Up

When you purchase resistance bands, they usually come with a set of exercises. Any of those can be substituted or added to these stations. These stations can also be added to any skill stations from the previous chapter.

Cardio-Jump

Grades
3-6

Skills
Cardiovascular fitness and endurance, coordination and flexibility

Get Started
This lesson does not have very many stations, but it is guaranteed to provide a good physical workout.

Long Rope

Equipment Long jump ropes (2)

Preparation Place the two ropes in the designated station area. Have two students stand 10 to 15 feet apart and turn the jump rope. Have the other students in the group take turns jumping, then turning the rope.

Objective Students turn the long rope with a partner. Students also practice various long-rope tricks.

Double Dutch

Equipment Long ropes (2)

Preparation Have two students turn the long ropes while the other students take turns jumping into the two moving ropes.

Objective Students will take turns practicing turning and jumping into double dutch ropes.

Individual Rope

Equipment Jump ropes (1 for each student in the group)

Preparation Lay the ropes in the designated station area.

Objective Students practice various rope skills such as skipping, jumping on one foot, crossing the rope, and speed jumping as designated by the teacher.

Make It Count
The main goals for this lesson center on providing opportunities to encourage a cardiovascular workout and to improve coordination and jumping skills. The lesson does require a large room or gym.

Make It Safe

Be sure to stress jump rope safety rules. My rules are to keep your shoes tied, to jump only in your personal space, and to always watch out for other students' jump ropes. These simple rules cut down boo-boos caused by the jump ropes.

Change It Up

This lesson works best when accompanied by lively music. I like to play *The Best of the '50s* or a Beach Boys collection.

Championship Obstacle Course

Grades
K-6

Skills
Cardiovascular fitness and endurance, coordination and flexibility

Get Started
Who doesn't love an obstacle course? The key with this lesson is to first do each activity as a station before changing it to an obstacle course.

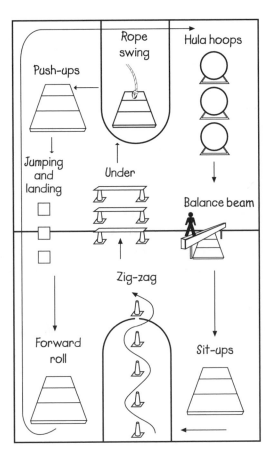

Key

Balance beam	Hula hoop w/Styrofoam holder	Mat
Climbing rope	Hurdle	Milk crate
Cone		

Hula Hoops

Equipment Hula hoops (3)
Styrofoam holders (6)

Preparation Stand each hula hoop on its side, using two Styrofoam holders per hoop.

Objective Students crawl through hula hoops.

Balance Beam

Equipment Balance beam (1)
Tumbling mat (1)

Preparation Place the balance beam away from walls and other objects. Lay the mat underneath the beam.

Objective Students walk across the balance beam without falling or starting over.

Sit-Ups

Equipment Tumbling mat (1)

Preparation Place the mat in the station area.

Objective Students perform 15 to 30 sit-ups.

Zig-Zag

Equipment Cones (5-7)

Preparation Place the cones in a straight line about 3 feet apart from one another.

Objective Students jog through the cones in a zig-zag pathway without stopping or walking.

Under

Equipment Hurdles (3)

Preparation Place the hurdles in a straight line about 2 feet from one another.

Objective Students crawl or drag themselves under the hurdles.

Rope Swing

Equipment Climbing rope (1)
Tumbling mat (1)

Preparation Place the mat under the rope.

Objective Students hold onto the rope and swing across the mat without touching the mat or letting go of the rope.

Push-Ups

Equipment Tumbling mats (or carpet squares) (1 for each student in the group)

Preparation Place the mats or carpet squares in the designated area.

Objective Students perform a designated number of push-ups.

Jumping and Landing

Equipment Carpet squares (3)
Low benches (or milk crates) (3)

Preparation Place the carpet squares carpet-side up on the floor, and place a bench or milk crate on each one. This helps to keep the benches or boxes from moving. Place them 3 feet from one another in a straight line.

Objective Students jump up on and down from each of the crates or boxes.

Forward Roll

Equipment Tumbling mat (or wedge mat) (1)

Preparation Place the mat in the designated station area.

Objective Students do a forward roll using correct form on the mat.

Make It Count

When I go through and explain each of the activities, I do not mention that we are doing an obstacle course. Students sometimes have a hard time understanding the concepts of doing one station then moving to the next one. After I explain all of the activities, I then inform my students that this is an obstacle course. I tell them that as soon as they finish one station, they may move directly to the next station without stopping.

Make It Safe

Use tumbling mats whenever it is necessary. Also explain to your students what behavior is acceptable when waiting to do each station of the obstacle course.

Change It Up

These activities are designed to use the entire gym. Therefore, if you have extra room, feel free to include other stations from this book with your obstacle course, or be creative and invent a few new ones.

Healthy Heart Circuits

Grades
2-4

Skills
Cardiovascular fitness and endurance, cross-curricular study, teamwork and cooperation

Get Started
I use this circuit during the month of Feburary, National Heart Month. This lesson allows students to walk through the circulatory system. I have found that it is best to use all red and blue equipment.

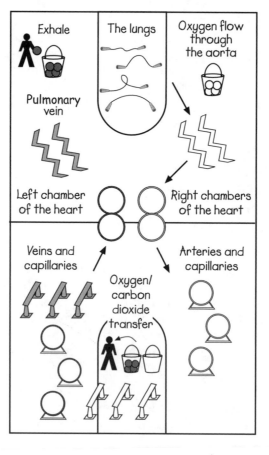

Key

 Bucket
 Cone
Grey and white hula hoop w/Styrofoam stand

 Red and blue hurdles
Jump rope
Red and blue hula hoops

 Red and blue mat (accordian-style)

 Red and blue medium balls

Red represents the arteries; blue represents the veins. In the equipment section, I designate which are red and which are blue. If the suggested colors are not available, this series is still worth doing with a clear lesson plan that explains which are arteries and which are veins.

The Lungs

Equipment   Jump ropes (3-5)

Preparation   Place the jump ropes at the beginning of the circuit. Explain to students that the jump ropes represent the lungs taking in oxygen.

Objective   Students jump rope in the lungs, 5-10 jumps.

Oxygen Flow Through the Aorta

Equipment   Box (or bucket) (1)
Red balls (or beanbags) (20-25)
Red tumbling mats (2)

Preparation   Stand the mats on their sides accordian-style, creating a tunnel. Place all of the balls in the box, and set the box at the beginning of the tunnel.

Objective   Each student picks up a red ball or beanbag, which represents oxygen, and carries it through the aorta and on to the next station.

Right Chambers of the Heart

Equipment   Red hula hoops (2)
Duct tape

Preparation   Tape the two hula hoops to the floor.

Objective   Students continue carrying the red balls while stepping through each of the hula hoops.

Arteries and Capillaries

Equipment   Red hula hoops (2 or 3)
Styrofoam holders (4 or 6)
Red low hurdles (2 or 3)

Preparation   Place the hula hoops in their stands, arranging them in a row 2 to 3 feet from one another. Continue in the straight path with the hurdles placed in a row 2 to 3 feet apart.

Objective   Students continue to carry the oxygen—first moving through the round arteries, then squeezing through the even smaller capillaries.

Oxygen/Carbon Dioxide Transfer

Equipment   Boxes (or buckets) (2)
Blue balls (or beanbags) (20-25)

Preparation   Set an empty box out first, followed by the other box with all of the blue balls in it.

Objective   Students drop the red ball into the box and then pick up a blue ball.

Veins and Capillaries

Equipment   Blue hula hoops (2 or 3)
Styrofoam stands (4 or 6)
Low blue hurdles (2 or 3)

Preparation   Place the hula hoops in their stands, arranging them in a row 2 to 3 feet from each other. Continue in a straight path with the hurdles placed in a row 2 to 3 feet apart.

Objective   Students continue to carry the carbon dioxide— first moving through the round veins, then squeezing into the even smaller capillaries back toward the heart.

Left Chamber of the Heart

Equipment   Blue hula hoops (2)
Duct tape

Preparation   Tape the two hula hoops next to the red hula hoops.

Objective   Students carry the carbon dioxide through the two left chambers of the heart.

Pulmonary Vein

Equipment   Blue tumbling mats (2)

Preparation   Stand the mats on their sides accordian-style, creating a tunnel.

Objective   Students continue carrying the carbon dioxide back through the lungs.

Exhale

Equipment   Large box (or bucket) (1)

Preparation   Place the box at the end of the tunnel.

Objective   Students deposit the blue balls into the box.

Make It Count

This circuit is set up in a circle. Usually, about five or six students can start at the same time, then you can start more when that group gets about halfway through. This activity does require a lot of explanation and discussion. I also stop the students while they are in the circuit and have them tell me where they are in the circulatory system. This is also a good opportunity for them to ask questions. This activity is great to do in February (National Heart Month), or when students are studying the circulatory system or participating in Jump Rope for Heart.

Make It Safe

You may feel it necessary to place additional mats under the hurdles and hula hoops. Remind your students that this is not a race and that they need to be careful as they travel through the various parts of the circuit.

Change It Up

The overall circuit can be made as big as you would like by increasing the number of mats, hula hoops, and hurdles at each station.

Upper-Body Toning

Grades
3-6

Skills
Cardiovascular fitness and endurance, strength training and conditioning

Get Started
Use these activities as a quick fitness warm-up before a lesson or as an entire workout lesson.

Pull-Ups

Equipment Chin-up bar (1)

Preparation Place the bar at the appropriate height.

Objective Students successfully perform two to five pull-ups.

Arm Curls

Equipment One-yard strips of resistance band (1 for each student in the group)

Preparation Have each student hold the band at one end with one of their hands and place the other end under one of their feet. Remind them to keep their elbows in close to their body as they slowly bring their hands up toward the shoulder.

Objective Students successfully perform 10 to 15 curls on each arm.

Push-Ups

Equipment Tumbling mats (or carpet squares) (1 for each student in the group)

Preparation Place the mat in the designated tumbling area.

Objective Students successfully perform 5 to 10 push-ups.

Rope Climb

Equipment Climbing rope (1)
Tumbling mat (1)

Preparation Place the tumbling mat under the rope.

Objective Students attempt to climb the rope without starting over.

Crab Push-Ups

Equipment Tumbling mat (1)

Preparation Place the mat in the designated station area.

> ***Objective*** Students successfully perform 10 to 15 crab push-ups using correct form.

Make It Count

Provide enough equipment at each station so that every student has something to do. Play lively music and have the students change stations when the music stops. Consider making a tape with music playing for two to three minutes followed by 30 seconds of silence.

Make It Safe

Allow time at the beginning of class for stretching. Encourage your students to continue stretching between each activity.

Change It Up

Include some nontraditional fitness activities, such as basketball dribbling, rope jumping, or football throwing. All these activities strengthen arm muscles.

Lower-Body Strengthening

Grades
3-6

Skills
Cardiovascular fitness and endurance, strength training and conditioning

Get Started

This lesson focuses on strengthening the muscles in the legs and lower body. Combined with basic anatomy, these are great exercises to emphasize the numerous muscles located in the lower body.

Sit-Ups

Equipment Tumbling mat (1)

Preparation Place the tumbling mat in the designated station area.

Objective Students do 30 to 50 sit-ups.

Leg Lifts

Equipment Tumbling mat (1)

Preparation Place the mat in the designated station area.

Objective Students lie on the mat and do 20 to 30 leg lifts with each leg.

Bicycle

Equipment Tumbling mat (1)

Preparation Place the mat in the designated station area.

Objective Students lie on the mat and do continuous bicycle pedals.

Leg Lunges

Equipment Cones (2)

Preparation Place the cones 10 to 15 feet away from each other in a straight line.

Objective Students take giant lunge steps from one cone to the other and back.

Step-Ups

Equipment Step benches (1 for each student in the group)

Preparation Space the steps away from each other in the station area.

Objective At their own step bench, each student follows this routine: Step up with the left foot; step up with the right foot; step down with the left, then down with the right. Students continue this until it is time to change stations.

Make It Count

Provide enough space and equipment so that all of the students can be doing something all of the time. Make the transitions short and quick so that your students are continuously moving and getting a good cardiovascular workout.

Make It Safe

Before beginning these stations, take the time to go over each exercise. Stress to the students how important it is to do all of the exercises correctly. This small investment of time reduces the number of injuries and provides maximum benefit to the students.

Change It Up

To provide additional stations, try adding jogging, jumping rope, or another cardiovascular exercise. This activity can be used as a quick fitness warm-up. Have the students stay at each activity about 30 seconds, then have them move on to the next station. They should be able to do all of the stations in about five minutes.

Warm-Up and Cool-Down Stretching

Grades   **Skills**
2-6   Coordination and flexibility

Get Started
Most professional athletes know that stretching is an integral part of any athletic activity; unfortunately, stretching is not a priority for many elementary or middle school athletes. Use this lesson to stress the importance of stretching to improve performance and reduce the risk of injury. Be sure to emphasize good technique.

Toe Touches
Equipment   No equipment necessary.

Preparation Have students stand with legs straight and together while trying to touch their toes with their hands. An advanced stretch is to cross their feet and then try to reach and touch their toes.

Objective   Students hold the stretch for 20 seconds.

Shoulder Stretch
Equipment   No equipment necessary.

Preparation Have each student stretch one arm across the chest and under the chin. Then have each place the opposite hand on that elbow and push the arm under the chin.

Objective   Students hold the stretch for 20 seconds and repeat with the other arm, doing each shoulder three times.

Lower Back Strech
Equipment   No equipment necessary.

Preparation Have students sit on the floor in the pike position. Have the students slowly reach to touch their toes without bending their knees.

Objective   Students hold each stretch for 20 seconds and repeat.

Quadriceps Stretch
Equipment   No equipment necessary.

Preparation Have students stand on one of their feet and hold onto one of their ankles with one of their hands.

Have them slowly pull their ankles slightly backward and toward the front of the body while keeping their knees together.

Objective Students hold the stretch for 20 seconds and repeat three times on each leg.

Calves

Equipment No equipment necessary.

Preparation Have students stand with both hands on a wall. Have them step back with one of their feet and have each push that heel down to the floor.

Objective Students hold this stretch for 20 seconds and then repeat three times with each foot.

Make It Count
After doing all of the stretches together as a group, use these stations as a quick fitness warm-up at the beginning of class. Set the correct mood by playing soft, soothing music. It may be helpful to place pictures of the stretch in each of the station areas.

Make It Safe
Reinforce the *stretch rule,* not the *bounce rule,* for each stretching exercise.

Change It Up
As your students successfully master these stretches, begin adding new and more challenging ones.

CHAPTER 5

Themes

Here's your chance to be the talk of the school. These lessons walk you through step by step as you transform your gymnasium into a creepy *Haunted Gym*, wild and wooly *Big Top*, or even a shimmering *Winter Wonderland*. The thematic lessons in this chapter are perfect springboards for other holidays and special events. Remember: Keep checking that calendar and looking ahead—you never know what inspiration might be peeking right around the corner.

Halloween Frights

Grades
K-6

Skills
Fundamental concepts, sports skills, teamwork and cooperation

Get Started
This Halloween lesson can be done in any large space, such as a gymnasium or commons room.

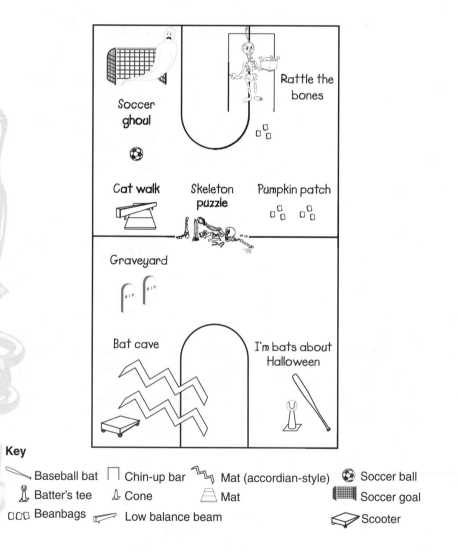

Key

- Baseball bat
- Batter's tee
- Beanbags
- Chin-up bar
- Cone
- Low balance beam
- Mat (accordian-style)
- Mat
- Soccer ball
- Soccer goal
- Scooter

Bat Cave

Equipment   Tumbling mats (4)
Scooter (1)
Parachute (1) (or several large blankets)

Preparation   Fold each mat accordion style to create a tunnel. Cover the tunnel with parachute or blankets.

Objective   Students take turns lying on their bellies and pushing themselves with their arms through the tunnel.

Graveyard

Equipment   Tumbling mats (2)
Funny graveyard signs (4)

Preparation   Lay the tumbling mats in the station area and place the graveyard signs around the mat. Instruct students to do as many sit-ups as they can in one minute.

Objective   Students perform a set number of sit-ups.

Cat Walk

Equipment   Low balance beam (1)
Tumbling mat (1)

Preparation   Place the balance beam away from walls and other equipment. Place a mat under the balance beam.

Objective   Students walk across the balance beam three out of five times without falling.

Soccer Ghoul

Equipment   Soccer goal (1)
Soccer ball (1)
Duct tape

Preparation   Place the goal against a wall. Apply a tape line to the floor 10 to 12 feet in front of the goal.

Objective   Students kick the soccer ball into the net three out of five times.

Skeleton Puzzle

Equipment   Poly-plastic skeleton puzzle (1)

Preparation   Lay the puzzle pieces on the station area.

Objective   Students put the puzzle together before it becomes time to move to the next station.

Rattle the Bones

Equipment   Plastic skeleton (1)
Beanbag (or similar sized ball) (1)
Chin-up bar (or basketball goal) (1)

Preparation   Hang the skeleton from a chin-up bar or basketball goal. Tape a line 10 to 12 feet in front of the
skeleton.

Objective   Students hit the skeleton using the correct throw
five out of seven times.

Pumpkin Patch

Equipment   Orange beanbags (1 for every 2 students in the
group)

Preparation   Have students stand 5 to 7 feet from a partner and
toss a beanbag using a correct underhand throw.

Objective   Students accurately throw a beanbag with correct
underhand style five out of seven times.

I'm Bats About Halloween

Equipment   Plastic batter's tee (1)
Plastic bat (1)
Plastic ball (1)

Preparation   Place tee 5 to 10 feet from a wall. Put the ball on
the tee. Have each student hit the ball off the tee
toward the wall.

Objective   Students hit the ball off of the tee with the bat.

Make It Count

This lesson is great for additional practice of underhand/overhand
throwing, kicking, and striking.

Make It Safe

I often allow older students to supervise the stations. Young students
can get quite involved as well, and the extra supervision is always
helpful.

Change It Up

To make the lesson even better try dimming the lights, wearing
costumes, and playing scary music.

Christmas Cheers

Grades
K-6

Skills
Cardiovascular fitness and endurance, team-work and cooperation

Get Started
Ho, ho, ho! Santa's coming. Bring in the holiday cheer with this lesson. It is packed with imaginative holiday activities.

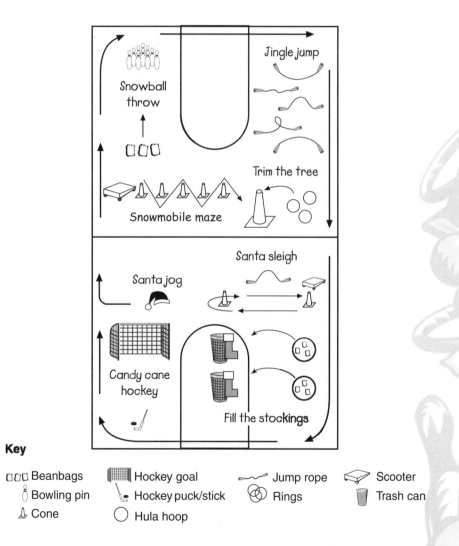

Key

ꝏ Beanbags	Hockey goal	Jump rope	Scooter
ꝏ Bowling pin	Hockey puck/stick	Rings	Trash can
Cone	Hula hoop		

Candy Cane Hockey

Equipment   Red hockey stick (1)
White masking tape
Hockey goal (1)
Hockey puck (1)

Preparation   Put a hockey goal next to a wall. Place a tape line about 10 feet in front of the goal. Wrap the red hockey stick with the white tape to create a striped effect.

Objective   Students use the hockey stick to push the puck into the goal three out of five times.

Santa Jog (or the Reindeer Run)

Equipment   Santa hats (or reindeer antlers) (4 or 5)
Cones (if necessary)

Preparation   If necessary, use the cones to define a jogging area that can serve as the track for the race.

Objective   Students jog around the gym or a designated area wearing Santa hats or reindeer antlers.

Snowmobile Maze

Equipment   Scooter (1)
Cones (5)

Preparation   Place the cones in a straight line about 3 feet apart from one another.

Objective   Students lie on their bellies and use their hands to zig-zag through the cones and back without touching cones.

Snowball Throw

Equipment   Plastic bowling pins (6-10)
Beanbags (3)
Duct tape

Preparation   Set the bowling pins up in a triangle formation. Place a tape mark on the floor 5 to 7 feet away and lay the beanbags on the tape mark.

Objective   Students knock down at least four bowling pins, three out of five times.

Jingle Jump

Equipment   Jump ropes (5 or 6)
Twist ties (10-12)
Large jingle bells (30)

Preparation To attach jingle bells to jump rope, tie a loose knot in the jump rope near the handles. Put three jingle bells on a twist tie. Slide one end of the twist tie through the knot and twist the ends of the ties together.

Objective Students jump rope 10 to 15 times in a row.

Trim the Tree

Equipment Large traffic cone (1)
Green construction paper
Clear tape
Rings (3)

Preparation Wrap the cone with green paper and tape the paper in place. Set the cone in the station area. Place a tape line on the floor 5 to 7 feet away from the cone.

Objective Students stand on the tape line and toss the three rings onto the cone five out of seven times.

Santa's Sleigh

Equipment Scooter (1)
Jump rope (1)
Cones (2)

Preparation Place the two cones 10 to 12 feet away from each other. Place the scooter and jump rope at one of the cones. Have one student be the Santa and sit on their knees on a scooter. Have the other partner be the reindeer, putting the jump rope around their waist.

Have the Santa grab the handles and be pulled by the reindeer to the other cone and back.

Objective Students take turns being Santa and the reindeer.

Fill the Stockings

Equipment Small trash can (or bucket) (1)
Foam balls (or beanbags) (3)
Red poster board, cut in the shape of a stocking (1)
Clear tape

Preparation Tape the poster board stocking onto the front of the small trash can and place a tape line on the floor 5 to 7 feet away. Lay the foam balls on the line.

Objective The students toss each foam ball or bean bag into the bucket five out of seven times.

Make It Count
Even though this is a fun lesson, be sure to stress the importance of doing each skill correctly.

Make It Safe
Watch the hockey station. I remind my class not to raise the stick above their knees. Also, *Santa's Sleigh* can be harmful to fingers and toes if they are not kept up on the scooter.

Change It Up
The possibilities are endless. Decorate with Christmas lights; play Christmas music; bring in all your old Christmas decorations and display them in the gym. If your school frowns on religious activities, change the name to *Happy Holiday* stations.

Winter Wonderland

Grades	Skills
K-6	Sports skills, strength training and conditioning, teamwork and cooperation

Get Started

This is a great lesson to break up the wintertime blahs. In our area, it doesn't snow enough to enjoy outdoor snow activities, so this is a great way to pretend.

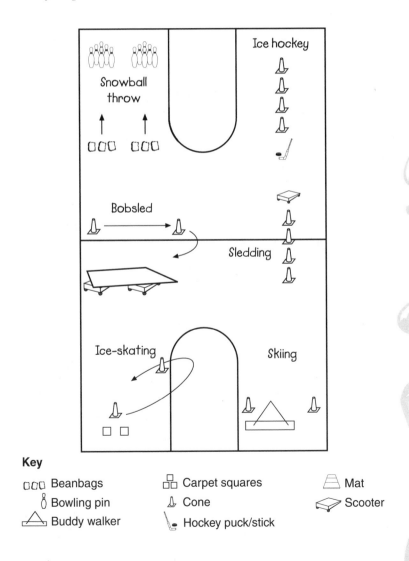

Key

▢▢▢ Beanbags	⊞ Carpet squares	△ Mat
⚬ Bowling pin	⚬ Cone	Scooter
◭ Buddy walker	⬣ Hockey puck/stick	

Snowball Throw

Equipment   Beanbags (3)
Plastic bowling pins (6-10)
Duct tape

Preparation   Set up the bowling pins in a triangle formation.
Place a tape line on the floor 5 to 10 feet away.
Place the beanbags on the tape line.

Objective   Students knock down at least four bowling pins.

Ice Hockey

Equipment   Cones (4 or 5)
Hockey stick (1)
Puck (1)

Preparation   Set the cones out in a straight line about 3 feet
from one another. Place the hockey stick and puck
at the beginning cone.

Objective   Students dribble a hockey puck through cones
without hitting the cones.

Sledding

Equipment   Scooter (1)
Cones (4)

Preparation   Place the four cones in a line 3 feet from one
another. Put the scooter at the starting cone.

Objective   Students either lie on their bellies or sit on their
bottoms and push themselves through a maze of
cones without touching the cones.

Skiing

Equipment   Set of Buddy Walkers (1)
Cones (2)

Preparation   Place the cones 5 to 7 feet away from each other.
Put the Buddy Walkers at the starting cone.

Objective   Students use the Buddy Walkers to travel to the
other cone and back.

Ice-Skating

Equipment Carpet squares (2)
Cones (2)

Preparation Lay the carpet squares, carpet-side down at one of the cones.

Objective Students stand on two carpet squares and slide to the other cone with speed and accuracy.

Bobsled

Equipment Folding tumbling mats (2)
Scooters (2)
Cones (2)

Preparation Lay two folded tumbling mats on top of the two scooters to make a bobsled. Park the bobsled at one of the cones and place the other 15 feet away.

Objective One student sits on the bobsled, and another student pushes the bobsled to the other cone and then back.

Make It Count

This lesson doesn't lend itself very well to assessing skills; however, by adding an unrelated station, the teacher could assess fitness skills, such as sit-ups or pull-ups.

Make It Safe

I like to stay moving during this lesson. The bobsled often needs readjusting, and sometimes students need help at the skiing station.

Change It Up

To add atmosphere and make the stations more challenging, have your students wear mittens and scarves. Don't forget those extra winter decorations—inflatable snowmen, snowflakes on the wall, and snow shovels.

The Zoo

Grades   **Skills**
K-2   Cross-curricular study, fundamental concepts

Get Started
Do your students act like they are wild animals? Well, turn the gym into a zoo. Your students are still practicing many basic movement and coordination skills. Just make sure they know who the zoo-keeper is!

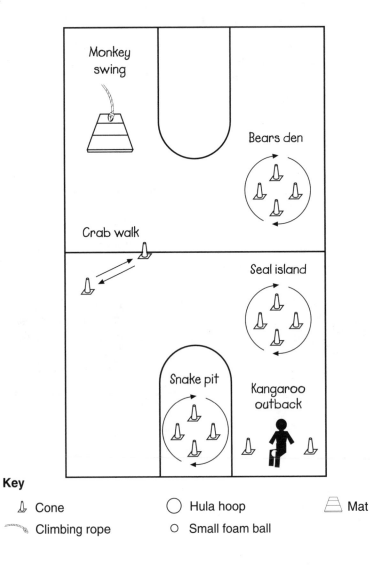

Key

🔱 Cone   ◯ Hula hoop   ⬠ Mat

〰 Climbing rope   ○ Small foam ball

Bear's Den
Equipment Cones (4)

Preparation Arrange the cones to make a 6-foot square.

Objective Students place both hands on the ground and walk with slightly bent knees around the outside of the den.

Seal Island
Equipment Cones (4)

Preparation Arrange the cones to make a 6-foot square.

Objective Students lie on the ground, then push their body up and walk on their hands, dragging themselves around the shore of the island.

Kangaroo Outback
Equipment Cones (2)
Small foam ball (1)

Preparation Place the two cones 10 feet away from each other.

Objective Students hold the ball between their knees, then jump from the starting cone to the other cone and back without dropping the ball.

Snake Pit
Equipment Cones (4)

Preparation Arrange the cones to make a 6-foot square.

Objective Students lie on their bellies and slither like a snake around the outside of the pit.

Crab Walk
Equipment Cones (2)

Preparation Place cones in straight line 6 feet apart.

Objective Students walk on their hands and feet with their bellies facing the ceiling around the two cones without letting their bottoms touch the ground.

Monkey Swing
Equipment Climbing rope (1)
Tumbling mat (1)

Preparation Place the tumbling mat under the rope.

Objective Students climb the rope without stopping and starting over.

Make It Count
Encourage your students to use their imaginations. Let them make animal sounds and add their own unique touches.

Make It Safe
Remind your students to take turns at each station. Place a tumbling mat under the climbing rope and consider having an adult there at all times.

Change It Up
Consult your students for alternative animals and their movements. Enhance your lesson by using music and by providing animal masks or tails. This can be done in conjunction with a science project.

Mother Goose

Grades
K-2

Skills
Cross-curricular study, fundamental concepts

Get Started
Children love nursery rhymes and song games. This is a great station
to put words and actions together for added fun.

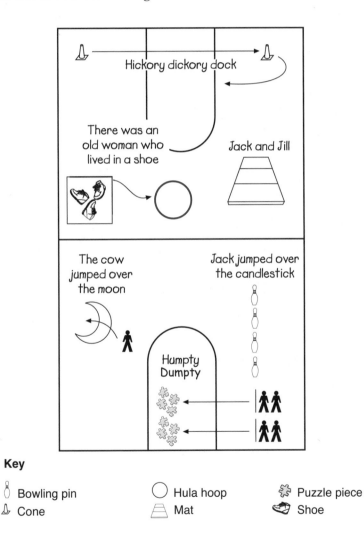

Key

⚲ Bowling pin   ◯ Hula hoop   ✲ Puzzle piece
⚷ Cone   △ Mat   👟 Shoe

Hickory Dickory Dock—The Mouse Ran Up the Clock

Equipment   Cones (2)

Preparation   Place the cones 15 to 20 feet from each other.

Objective   Students run from one cone to another or around the gym in relay style.

Jack and Jill

Equipment   Tumbling mat (1)

Preparation   Place the tumbling mat in the designated tumbling area.

Objective   Students do three forward rolls on a tumbling mat using correct form and posture.

Jack Jumped Over the Candlestick

Equipment   Plastic bowling pins (3-5)

Preparation   Place the pins in a straight line about 3 feet apart from one another.

Objective   Students jump over each of the bowling pins without touching the top or sides of the pins.

Humpty Dumpty

Equipment   Humpty Dumpty puzzles with 10 to 25 pieces (2)

Preparation   Place the puzzles 10 to 20 feet from the starting line.

Objective   The students form two relay teams. Each student takes a turn running to get one puzzle piece and returning it to the starting line. The team that gets the puzzle together first, wins.

The Cow Jumped Over the Moon

Equipment   White masking tape

Preparation   Create different size moons on the floor using the tape.

Objective   Students leap over a moon on the floor without touching the moon.

There Was an Old Woman Who Lived in a Shoe

Equipment Old shoes (3)
Hula hoop (or laundry basket) (1)
Duct tape

Preparation Make a starting line using the tape. Place the hula hoop or basket 7 to 10 feet away from the starting line. Place a variety of old shoes at the starting line.

Objective Students will take turns using an underhand throw to toss the old shoes into the hula hoop or large basket three out of five times.

Make It Count
Place a copy of each of the nursery rhymes at the station. Allow enough time at each station for your students to read the nursery rhymes and do the activity. This would be a great lesson to do during National Read Across America Week.

Make It Safe
Make sure all of your students have their shoes tied before beginning any of the stations. I have found that staying close to the *Jack and Jill* station prevents injuries and close calls.

Change It Up
If your kindergarten classes have upper-grade "buddies," this would be a great activity to do together. The older students could read the nursery rhymes and help with each of the stations.

Under the Big Top

Grades
K-2

Skills
Coordination and flexibility, fundamental concepts, strength training and conditioning

Get Started
Kids love to go to the circus. Why not create one in your gym? This time, your students get to participate and not just watch from the stands.

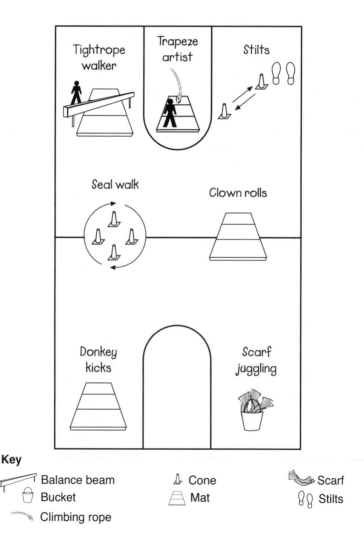

Key

Balance beam	Cone	Scarf
Bucket	Mat	Stilts
Climbing rope		

Tightrope Walker

Equipment Balance beam (1)
Tumbling mats (1 or 2)

Preparation Place the balance beam in a safe area, away from walls and other equipment. Position the mats under the balance beam to protect from injury if a student falls.

Objective The student walks forward, backward, and sideways across the beam without falling.

Trapeze Artist

Equipment Climbing rope (1)
Tumbling mat (1)

Preparation Place the tumbling mat under the rope.

Objective Students attempt to climb the rope.

Stilts

Equipment Set of stilts (1)
Cones (2)

Preparation Place the cones 7 feet from each other. Put the stilts at the beginning cone.

Objective Students walk on the stilts from one cone to the other and back without falling.

Clown Rolls

Equipment Tumbling mats (1 or 2)

Preparation Lay the mats in an area away from walls and other equipment.

Objective Students take turns doing a forward roll on the tumbling mat using correct form.

Scarf Juggling

Equipment Scarves (3 for each student at the station)
Bucket (or bowl) (1)

Preparation Place all of the scarves at the station in a bucket or bowl.

Objective Students practice scarf juggling.

Donkey Kicks

Equipment Tumbling mat (1)

Preparation Place the tumbling mat in the station area. Make sure it is not near walls or other equipment.

Objective   Students practice handstands by doing donkey kicks on the tumbling mat.

Seal Walk

Equipment   Cones (4)

Preparation   Arrange the cones to make a 6-foot square.

Objective   Students drag their body like a seal.

Make It Count

A lot of these stations complement tumbling and balance skills, making them a great addition to a tumbling unit.

Make It Safe

Several of these stations require tumbling mats in case of falls. These stations are a lot of fun, but additional adult supervision is ideal.

Change It Up

Occasionally parents dress as clowns and participate in the fun. Other ways to spice it up are to use helium balloons, play circus music, and make fun circus signs for each station.

Field Day

Grades
K-4

Skills
Cardiovascular fitness and endurance, coordination and flexibility, fundamental concepts, and sports skills

Get Started
Field days are perfect for bringing great weather and children together. This lesson is designed to do just that!

Individual Jump Rope

Equipment Jump ropes (1 for every child in the class)

Preparation Pick a station area that is blacktopped and relatively flat. Scatter the jump ropes in the area.

Objective Students use the jump ropes to practice basic skills. Teachers may wish to organize races or contests.

Toss Games

Equipment Different kinds of toss games (10-15): ring toss, horseshoes, beanbags, rings, balls

Preparation Place all of the toss games in a large area.

Objective Students use underhand throw to do ring tosses, hit various targets, or play horseshoes.

Big Clothes Relay

Equipment Sets of large clothes (2)
Hula hoops (2)

Preparation Divide the class into two teams. Place a set of very large clothes for each team in a hula hoop about 15 to 20 feet away.

Objective The teams compete in relay format to run down and put the clothes on, then run back to the line and take them off. The next person then puts them on and runs to the hula hoop to take them off. This cycle continues until everyone in the line has had a turn.

Frisbee Throw

Equipment Frisbee (1 for each child in the class)

Preparation Choose a large, grassy field and place the Frisbees in a box or crate.

Objective Students throw Frisbees in a designated area with a partner.

Racket Relay

Equipment   Tennis rackets (2)

Beanbags (2)

Wiffle balls (2)

Any other objects that can be balanced on the face of the racket (2 per object)

Cones (4)

Preparation   Place two cones for starting lines, then the other two about 20 feet away.

Divide the class into two teams and have them compete in a relay format.

Objective   The students carry various objects on a tennis racket face to a designated cone and back without dropping any of the objects.

Sack Races

Equipment   Burlap sacks (2)
Cones (4)

Preparation   Place two of the cones for starting cones, and place the other two cones 15 feet away. Divide the class into two relay teams.

Objective   The students compete in sack races or three-legged races.

Tug-of-War

Equipment   Tug-of-war rope (1)
Gloves (optional)

Preparation   Place the tug-of-war rope in a grassy flat area. Divide the class into two equal squads.

Objective   Students divide into teams and compete in tug-of-war.

Parachute

Equipment   Large parachute (1)

Preparation   Place the parachute in the gym or on a flat black-top area.

Objective   The entire class participates in teacher directed parachute games, such as Popcorn, Volcano, Igloo, and Mountain.

Scooter Races

Equipment Scooters (2)
Cones (4)

Preparation Place two cones as starting marks and the other
two about 20 to 30 feet away. Divide the class into
two teams.

Objective Students race each other.

Basketball Dribbling Relays

Equipment Basketballs (2)
Cones (2)

Preparation Place two cones as starting lines and the other
two cones 15 to 20 feet away.

Divide the class into several teams. This activity is
best if done on an outside basketball court or
inside in the gym.

Objective The class races several times. The teacher can
decide to vary the races each time.

Make It Count

Make sure that there are enough stations for every class to have
something to do at all times. Include any activity that your students
can do without your direct supervision. Make sure all of the teachers
know how to do all of the activities. Do not include games that may
be unfamiliar to your fellow classroom teachers. Our classes move
from one activity to another every 15 minutes, but other schools like
the teachers to move at their own discretion. I also provide all of the
teachers with a map and description of all of the stations.

Make It Safe

If you live in a warm climate, prepare your students for a hot day. We
advise parents to send sunscreen and let the students bring their own
drinks. We also provide a concession stand and sell drinks and ice
cream. We even had someone volunteer to make snow cones. Have
a first-aid kit available for those boo-boos and scratches.

Change It Up

Other activities that we have included in the past are face painting,
sidewalk chalk, and dancing. Think of outdoor, summer-camp-
type activities—perhaps even dare to think of something old and
classic.

CHAPTER

6

Stretches, Tags, and Quick Skills

This last chapter is a peek at the ideas I use on a weekly basis. They are ideal suggestions for days when both you and your students need a quick and fun break from the everyday routine. The stretches are favorites of the younger ones while the tags and quick skills rev up the older ones and help burn off extra energy. All of these exercises also are great refreshers to lessons using skills that students haven't practiced for a while. Enjoy!

Zoo Stretches

I call these *Zoo Stretches*. To make the most of the fun, I make large posters out of poster board or newsprint with the pictures of the animals listed below and hang them on the wall. After practicing the stretches together as a group, the students can eventually do them on their own or with a student leader. If the stretches are done in the following order, the students go from standing to sitting. Sometimes the students can even help think of new animal stretches.

Giraffe
The students stretch tall with their hands over their heads, then down to the floor with knees slightly bent. Repeat several times.

Elephant
Students put their hands together to make a trunk, then slowly move their arms from side to side.

Flamingo
Students stand on one foot while holding the other foot behind their bottoms. Repeat with the other foot.

Caterpillar
Students sit in a pike position and hold on to their feet or ankles. They then slowly bend their knees and bring their feet in toward the body and back out again.

Butterfly
Ask the students what a caterpillar turns into—a butterfly. Students put the bottom of their feet together and gently push their knees towards the floor. Instruct them not to bounce.

Seal
Students lie on their bellies with their hands under their shoulders. They then straighten their arms and lift their chests off the ground.

Owl
While sitting cross-legged, the students move their heads from side to side and stretch their wings.

Tag! You're It

The Gingerbread Man Tag
Read the story *The Gingerbread Man*. Afterward, assign the following parts: the Little Old Woman, the Little Old Man, the Cow, the Mowers, the Thratchers. They are the taggers. The remaining students are the Gingerbread Men. When the Gingerbread Men are tagged, they have to sit in a designated area. When all the Gingerbread Men have been tagged, choose new taggers.

Thankful Tag
Select an appropriate Thanksgiving book. Read it to your students. Discuss what we have to be thankful for. To play *Thankful Tag*, select two to four students to be taggers. When the students are tagged, they have to tell the teacher something they are thankful for. The teacher can either write these things on a board or on a large piece of paper. Select new taggers often and show the students all the things we are thankful for.

The Big Brag
This is a great closing activity and is inspired by the great Dr. Seuss book *The Big Brag*. The book is humorous and makes a great point about how bragging really makes people look. This activity is best used when discussing classroom rules, teamwork, cooperation, and fair play.

Wipe Out-and Other Quick Ideas

Introduce your students to the song "Wipe Out." Most "Wipe Out" songs last about four minutes, and it is best to use a version without too many words. Point out to the students that there are two parts to this song—a drum section and guitar section. The drum section is Part A, and the guitar section is Part B. Assign an activity to do during each part. Examples are below.

Individually

Part A
Run.

Part B
Walk.

With a Partner

Part A
One person dribbles a ball while the other jogs.

Part B
The partners pass the ball between them.

This activity can be used with all your teaching skills or just as a fitness activity.

Cardiovascular Motivators

I had a local manufacturer make the following stickers for my classes to represent the various fun runs we do in class. I use the stickers as rewards and acknowledgements of accomplishments.

The September Shuffle

The Goblin Gallop

Turkey Trot

Reindeer Run

I Ran a Mile for a Healthy Heart

March Marathon

I Can Do Sit-Ups

I Can Do Pull-Ups

I Can Jump Rope

Jumping Books

Younger grades have a hard time jumping rope for entire class period. They tend to get frustrated and bored with the activity. There are several books available that are good to use to break up the class time: *The Jump Book, The Up Book,* and *Norma Jean, the Jumping Bean.*

Abs, Abs, Abs

In this quick exercise, students find a partner and sit in a bent-knee, sit-up position facing each other. The students then hook their feet together for support. Use the following pattern, or you can even make up one of your own: pat knees, clap hands, pat partner's hands, snap–snap. Students lower their torso to the ground during the snap–snap, then back up to pat their legs. Use a great, upbeat song like "Hit Me With Your Best Shot" by Pat Benatar or "Eye of the Tiger" by Survivor. Your students get about three to five minutes of sit-ups, and hopefully, they have a good time, too.

About the Author

Maggie C. Burk is a physical educator who has taught elementary physical education for eight years. She received her master of arts degree in adapted physical education from Tennessee Technical University in 1994. She is a member of the Tennesee Association of Physical Education, Recreation and Dance.